FAHREN HYPE 9/11
Companion Book

UNRAVELING THE TRUTH ABOUT FAHRENHEIT 9/11 & MICHAEL MOORE

"The perfect complement to the FahrenHYPE 9/11 DVD"

EDITED BY
LEE TROXLER

www.fahrenHYPE911.com

LEE TROXLER

www.fahrenHYPE911.com

ISBN 0-9762187-052495

THIS began as a private project and will, hopefully, continue that way. We take pride in having produced the *FahrenHYPE 9/11* movie and this companion book without funding assistance from any political organization. Our objectives from the outset have been to provoke debate, to help the country move beyond the polarization that has hardened opinions, and to achieve a little clarity on the great issues facing our nation.

We wish we had started sooner, but at least we started. And we could not have completed anything at all without the kind and generous assistance of many wonderful people. We wish to thank, and encourage you to thank:

ANN COULTER – Her latest book is Treason: Liberal Treachery From the Cold War to the War on Terrorism

DAVID FRUM – His latest book is AN END TO EVIL: How to Win the War on Terror

FRANK GAFFNEY – Director of the Center for Security Policy

STEVE EMERSON – Author of American Jihad and Director of The Investigative Project

DAVE KOPEL – Director of the Independence Institute

PETER KING – A voice of reason and strength in Congress

ED KOCH – His many books and media appearances are not to be missed

DICK MORRIS – His next book is Because He Could

ZELL MILLER – His latest book is A National Party No More: The Conscience of a Conservative Democrat

RON SILVER – A talented actor and exemplar for us all

BILL SAMMON – His latest book is Misunderestimated: The President Battles Terrorism, John Kerry, and the Bush Haters

DAVID HARDY & JASON CLARKE – Authors of Michael Moore Is A Big Fat Stupid White Man

PETER DAMON – Courageous American Soldier

GWEN TOSE-RIGELL – A Great American Educator

JIM MOORE – His next book is Trapeze

The River Café in Brooklyn, New York

Savage Pictures in Salt Lake City

Many thanks to the gifted artists who provided their cartoon art. We urge you to support them, for they often labor in unfriendly climates. A review of 60 Michael Moore cartoons in the New York Times archives found not one suitable for this project—all 60 were biting, often vicious attacks on the President. Whether a Republican or Democrat holds the White House—the nation's paper of record should at least pretend toward balance, shouldn't it? We extend our appreciation to:

John Deering, Bill DeOre, Linda Eddy, Brian Farrington, Fox & Forkum, Steve Kelley, Mike Lester, Graeme MacKay, R.J. Matson, Glenn McCoy, Dan Murphy, Jeff Parker, John Pritchett, Dave Rosen, Juju Dandridge Suits, Gary Waltrip, and Larry Wright.

CONTENTS

CHAPTER 1   13
You Squeezed Into The Party, Like You Were Squeezing Onto A Yacht

CHAPTER 2   33
About Our Featured Guests

CHAPTER 3   39
Behind The Scenes With America's Leading Opinion Makers

CHAPTER 4   163
If *FahrenHYPE 9/11* Had Been A Fictional Spoof Like *Fahrenheit 9/11*

CHAPTER 5   169
A Selection From Michael Moore Is A Big Fat Stupid White Man

CHAPTER 6   181
This Man Speaks For The Democratic Party?

CHAPTER 7   187
Propaganda Tactics And *Fahrenheit 9/11*

CHAPTER 8   207
A Frame By Frame Deconstruction of *Fahrenheit 9/11*

CHAPTER 9   221
Why No Mention of Israel In Your Movie, Michael?

CHAPTER 10   227
Our First Film Review – Written While We Were Still Filming!

CHAPTER 1

YOU SQUEEZED INTO THE PARTY, LIKE YOU WERE SQUEEZING ONTO A YACHT

IT'S all about Michael. It's as if Carly's old song about Warren has been grotesquely refit for Michael. He's the suck-up du jour among the Hollywood hip and European has-beens. He's everywhere, shouting down anyone who disagrees with him, all the while calling for vigorous public debate. If he hasn't outgrown his own ego, it's only because his plentiful girth makes that an improbability. But today's media sensation is soon replaced, and Michael will soon be gone.

Not before a little honesty is hurled his way.

Michael has been likened by fellow filmmakers to Sinclair Lewis, and while Sinclair graduated from Yale and Michael couldn't make the college grade, they do share a gift that Sinclair said "so acutely annoyed American smugness that some thousands of my fellow citizens felt they must read these scandalous documents, whether they liked them or not."

Michael has also been likened to Hunter Thompson, again not incorrectly because weird Michael has turned pro by any capitalist definition –

making over $100 million on a movie means you've gone pro.

It is also fashionable these days to compare Michael's creative rough and tumble to Jonathan Swift. And when Michael modestly proposes that "there is no terrorist threat in this country, this is a lie," the listener has to admire the sheer unbridled creativity of the man.

The young and restless sure admire him. A recent *Rolling Stone* put him on the cover and called him "Mr. America". Reviewers who brand *Fahrenheit 9/11* an adolescent polemic or vicious broadside still praise it's signal achievement. They say he's fighting fire with fire, and whatever shadings of the truth or inaccuracies pale in comparison with those of his political foes.

Europe admires him. As Christopher Dickey wrote in *Newsweek*, "Moore reinforces all Europe's stereotypes about Americans: that they're violent, feckless and arrogant. But he also embodies the national bluntness that Europeans have come to admire. Plus, he's fat and wears a baseball cap."

Michael's book Stupid White Men sold more than a million copies in Germany and at one point three of his books were in the top four slots on the German bestseller lists. In dedicating the German edition of his book, he wrote that it was time for Germans to respect themselves again. Frankly, I prefer my Germans pacifist—inviting Germany to war is like inviting Michael to a Krispy Kream party—you don't want the sugar management problem.

So Michael is a likable court jester, a class clown, a big oaf who's not afraid to call a spade a heart. In the olden days when the court jester overstepped his bounds, he could expect to lose his head. These days, the bludgeon of choice is *honesty*.

And in the spirit of honesty, we can fairly call *Fahrenheit 9/11* a piece of entertainment, we can accurately call it propaganda or even polemic, but we can't call it documentary truth. The truth doesn't really interest Michael. It's not his game. As Michael told CNN's Lou Dobbs when asked about the accuracy of his movie, Michael responded "how can there be accuracy in

comedy?" Fair enough. If Michael wants to be judged as a comedian, then let the judging begin. Let him be compared to another comedian, say Bob Hope. The difference between the two was that Hope was actually funny, he was warm-hearted to all who met him, and he so dearly loved his country that he gave up every holiday to entertain our troops.

Michael's idea of entertaining the troops is claiming to have Abu Ghraib-type prison abuse footage and suggesting that all soldiers are disgraces to their country. Michael proves this by having the film crew that he embedded with U.S. troops film while our soldiers poke at an old drunk Iraqi laying in the street. Michael implies that this is Iraqi prisoner abuse. This is not courageous filmmaking, this is shameless profiteering. It cannot be rationalized away, except by a hypocrite. It cannot be taken seriously, except by gullible minds and lost souls. It cannot be given any credence whatsoever, except in a Coalition of the Damned.

THE PURPOSE OF THIS BOOK

In his movie Michael asked his audience to dream, in our movie *FahrenHYPE 9/11* we ask viewers to debate. Let's have a conversation about the big issues facing our nation. Let's fight a battle of ideas. And let's begin by setting the record straight about who Michael Moore really is and what he's trying to accomplish.

Spend even five minutes reading up on Michael and you'll discover that he has a long and comfortable relationship with deceit. He doesn't even tell the truth about where he was born. He calls home the hardscrabble town of Flint, Michigan. Yet he was born across the tracks in lily-white Davison, Michigan. It just degenerates from there.

He's calls himself a working class hero and he attacks corporations while flying around in corporate jets. He alternates between saying he speaks the truth and calling his work comedy—but there's no denying that he turns facts into fiction, truths into untruths. He positions himself as a courageous sword carrier of the people when in fact he cowers from anyone who could whip him in a debate.

One such person is Christopher Hitchens, a writer for *Vanity Fair*. On the subject of *Fahrenheit 9/11*, Hitchens wrote "To describe this film as dishonest and demagogic would almost be to promote those terms to the level of respectability. To describe this film as a piece of crap would be to run the risk of a discourse that would never again rise above the excremental. To describe it as an exercise in facile crowd-pleasing would be too obvious. *Fahrenheit 9/11* is a sinister exercise in moral frivolity, crudely disguised as an exercise in seriousness. It is also a spectacle of abject political cowardice masking itself as a demonstration of 'dissenting' bravery."

But a spectacle that a lot of Americans have accepted at face value. So we challenge Michael to get in the ring with us, slug it out with facts and all available evidence, and see who goes the distance…

ROUND 1 – MICHAEL'S DARKEST CONSPIRACY
BUSH IS IN THE POCKET OF SAUDI SHEIKS

If the Bush's and the al-Saud dynasty are locked in some vague plot to rule all of oildom, as Moore suggests with the subtly of a hammer, then there are questions left unanswered:

1. **Why didn't the Saudis join Bush's Coalition of the Willing?**
2. **Why didn't the Saudis let Bush locate our Iraq military HQ on Saudi sand?**
3. **Why didn't the Saudis stop Bush from demolishing Baghdad which buffers their regime from angry Shiite Muslims?**

Michael also suggests darkly that in the days following 9/11, the bin Laden clan scooted out of the country (1) at a time when all other air traffic was grounded and (2) on special transports arranged by Bush. The implication, of course, was that Bush knew these Saudis were up to no good and he was covering for them. The truth, made explicit and clear by the bipartisan 9/11 Commission Report, was that Michael got it wrong on both counts.

First, the 9/11 Commission reported that the flights left after the aircraft ban was lifted. Second, Bush knew nothing about the Saudi departure. Sole responsibility for authorizing the transports was made by Richard Clarke, as he himself testified. This is the same Richard Clark who was in charge of fighting terror under Clinton, and again under Bush, and Michael calls him the great heroic whistleblower. So the whole scene in *Fahrenheit 9/11* is shown to be a deceit wrapped in a prejudice stoked by ignorance, toppling all pretense of truth. This is the Michael M.O., as we see again and again…

ROUND 2 – MICHAEL'S WILDEST FANTASY
BUSH INVENTED THE WHOLE TERRORIST THREAT – IT'S A LIE!

You never quite know if Michael believes a word he's saying, or if he's like little Jack Horner of legend who wasn't a good boy at all, but a thief. Sticking his thumb in the pie, he pulled out the deed to a great Britain manor that was hidden amid the plums – it being common practice in those days to hide objects in pies. Today the con of choice is not theft but deception – fool enough of the people enough of the time and you get the manor on Lake Superior.

Michael would have people believe that somehow "Bush created the whole terrorist threat thing as part of a craven power grab." The terrorist threat is a lie, Michael says, dreamed up by Bush to:

> 1. **Line-up oil contracts for his buddies,**
> 2. **Prop-up his sagging presidency,**
> 3. **Cover-up his past ties to the Taliban,**
> 4. **Fill-in the blank – almost any claim is fair-game in Michael's world.**

AL QAEDA'S SECRET WEAPON: THE DIRTY, FAT, STUPID BOMB.

With thanks to John Pritchett

In Michael's world, the events of 9/11 either didn't matter ("you're three times more likely to struck by lightning than die from a terrorist attack," Michael tells us) or they did matter but we shouldn't be too hasty in doing anything about them ("bin Laden is innocent until proven guilty," Michael tells us).

Forget Bill Clinton saying in February 1998 that "we want to seriously diminish the threat posed by Iraq's weapons of mass destruction program" and his Secretary of State Albright adding that Hussein has "chosen to spend his money on building weapons of mass destruction and palaces for his cronies" and his National Security Advisor cementing the argument that Hussein "will use those weapons of mass destruction again."

Forget Teddy Kennedy saying "we have known for many years that Saddam Hussein is seeking and developing weapons of mass destruction."

Forget Al Gore saying "we know that he has stored secret supplies of biological and chemical weapons throughout his country."

Forget Hillary Clinton saying "he has also given aid, comfort, and sanctuary to terrorists, including al Qaeda members."

Forget John Kerry saying as late as January 2003 that "we need to disarm Saddam Hussein. He is a brutal, murderous dictator leading an oppressive regime ... the threat of Saddam Hussein with weapons of mass destruction is real."

Forget every Republican and Democrat of stature saying that we faced a terrible threat from Islamic Fascists and oppressors like Saddam who support or harbor terrorists. Forget all that. There's a new refrain in Michael's world: "George W. Bush is a deserter, an election thief, a drunk driver, a WMD liar, and a functional illiterate. And he poops his pants."

In Michael's world, it is only Michael who can contemptuously harangue or pillory anybody who disagrees with him. And this is the guy seated in a place of honor next to Jimmy Carter at the Democratic National Convention – the Democrats are listening to this clown. That's a truly frightening thought!

ROUND 3 – MICHAEL'S PACIFIST PREVARICATIONS
IRAQ UNDER SADDAM WAS ALL PUNCH AND ROSES

Hand it to Michael Moore. He made *Fahrenheit 9/11* into the vacation channel, treating us to carefree Baghdad – a top fun and sun spot before the U.S.
invaded. No ordinary filmmaker could have found such kids flying kites,
playing in playgrounds…except that they weren't in playgrounds. Look
closely at the film and you'll recognize one of Hussein's golden palaces,
you'll notice police centers…places where family members tended to dis-
appear, or get beaten by Saddam's thug sons.

Michael can't understand why we'd want to eliminate Saddam. In
Michael's world, this man posed no threat to us. This man wasn't a terrorist. This man never murdered an American. Well, let's spend a moment in
the real world…

> **- Every day for 10 year's Hussein fired surface-to-air missiles
> at U.S. planes patrolling no-fly zones that the United Nations
> had set up.**

> **- Hussein's brutal and unprovoked invasion of Kuwait killed
> quite a few Americans and Egyptians and Syrians and Brits
> when we came to Kuwait's defense.**

> **- Hussein boasted publicly that he paid cash rewards to
> Palestinians who strapped explosives on children's bodies for
> detonating in busy areas of Israel.**

> **- Hussein's secret police tried to murder an American
> President.**

> **- Hussein setup safe house after safe house for the world's
> ugliest terrorists… A safe house for Abu Nidal who ran terror-**

ist attacks on 20 countries and was so awful even the PLO wanted him dead. A safe house for Abdul Yasin who attacked the World Trade Center in the first 1993 attempt. A safe house for the man who pushed Leon Klinghoffer in his wheelchair over the side of the Achille Lauro.

- Hussein may or may not have been trying to obtain yellowcake to build 50 nuclear warheads a year from Niger. Some say he tried, some say he didn't. Put yourself in the position of the President – if a madman may be trying to obtain nuclear weapons, and those weapons could fall into the hands of terrorists sworn to destroy America, on what side do you err?

And even if Hussein wasn't a brutal dictator who exterminated as many as a million of his own people, even if every humanitarian impulse didn't say take him out, after 9/11 we had to take him out. After 9/11, Hussein's henchmen danced in the streets and called the attacks 'just the beginning.' And so after 9/11 we not only take out the terrorists but we take out anyone who sides with the terrorists against us...

ROUND 4 – MICHAEL'S ETERNAL SHAME
OUR SOLDIERS ARE DUMB REDNECKS WHO ABUSE
PRISONERS AND MURDER THE INNOCENT

It's not a thin line. It a big yawning chasm that separates patriotic dissent from shameful sedition. So when Michael tars every soldier with the excesses of a few, when Michael brands every soldier a duped idiot bent on rock music firing big guns at innocent children, when Michael claims to have footage of supposed heinous events and then we learn that he had nothing of the sort, that's crossing the chasm completely. And that carries a lifetime sentence of public shame.

In *Fahrenheit 9/11*, Michael shows footage of an apparently unconscious

With thanks to Larry Wright, The Detroit News

Iraqi on a stretcher, under a blanket, with some troops laughing at him. Various reviews have interpreted the Iraqi as a detainee, as wounded, or even as dead. On May 17, 2004, the *New York Times* reported that Moore was willing to give a sneak preview of some footage of the abuse: "Mr. Moore said he was considering making at least one sequence from the film available to the news media today after he presents it at the Cannes film festival: that of American soldiers laughing and taking pictures as they place hoods over Iraqi detainees, with one of them touching a prisoner's genitals through a blanket."

Pressed by the media, Michael conceded that "In fact, the soldiers had picked up an old man who had passed out drunk and they poked at his visible erection, covered by a blanket."

Fact is, war is hell and hellish things happen, as they most certainly did in Abu-Ghraib. And yes, this country has to hold its soldiers (if not its film-makers) to a higher standard—because it's the standard that we're fighting for. But when a few bad apples are held up as characteristic of the whole bunch, that is wrong, that is inaccurate, that is a particularly repugnant form of shame.

Is it any wonder that *Fahrenheit 9/11* is playing in the better Hezbollah and Hamas homes. These guys are used to seeing their own filmmakers make-up wild lies about the Americans. But never before have they seen an American quite so accomplished at deceit.

Then there's Michael's scene where Nazi-like military recruiters prey on poor minorities, trying to dupe them into joining the Army. How we could have poor black minorities getting duped by recruiters and dumb white rednecks doing the killing of innocents isn't exactly explained in Michael's movie. We can only guess about Michael's motivations for embarrassing the black community and defaming the white community.

ROUND 5 – MICHAEL'S MINDLESS MUSINGS
BUSH WAS UNABLE TO GET ANY LEGISLATION PASSED
PRIOR TO SEPTEMBER 11

No legislation? Well, let's see. Bush was able to convince both Houses of Congress to pass a tax cut. That sounds like major legislation. And while it's too early to judge the effects of this tax cut, we know that the Reagan tax cuts were a powerful enabler of the 1990s technology boom. And we can certainly hope that Bush's tax cut works similarly on the economy, while letting people keep more of the money they've earned. Bush accomplished other things as well, but our concern is not the President. Our concern is in showing that in manners large and small, Michael deceives, invents, prevaricates and panders. In short, lies. And what do you have when you build on a lie?

ROUND 6 – MICHAEL'S EMPTY ALLEGATIONS
BUSH BOMBED AFGHANISTAN NOT TO TAKE OUT TALIBAN,
BUT FOR OIL

Michael has so many positions on the initial war in Afghanistan, he makes John Kerry look positively resolute. But one of Michael's big themes is that all that "shock and awe" in the Afghanistan hills was about oil. By his logic, we have to conclude as follows: bin Laden and his Taliban protectors should have chosen to hide out in caves in Ecuador because we would never bomb there -- Ecuador has no oil. By Michael's logic, Bush bombed Afghanistan to make easy the construction of a natural gas pipeline for...cue evil music...oil giant Unocal.

You've probably heard others parrot this allegation. A master of propaganda knows that if you repeat a lie often enough, people start to believe it. In reality, Bush had supported Enron's plan to run pipes under the Caspian Sea and avoid Afghanistan. Clinton was the one backing a Unocal plan to run pipes through Afghanistan. But then, Unocal abandoned the idea even before Bush took office.

Even if the pipeline project was still alive, so what? How are we going to get the oil we use? Environmentalists have stopped us from exploring the arctic wilderness to its fullest potential—and maybe that's a good thing. Maybe that will force our government to commit with a little more imagination to the development of non-fossil fuels and move us toward the goal of zero emissions vehicles. But in the meantime, if we were to lose all oil imports it would toss this country into a Depression that would surely dwarf the 1920s. Nobody wants that, do they?

The whole truth of Afghanistan is that it's still an unstable place, and may forever be—given the intense tribal rivalries that exist there. But today, thanks to U.S. military forces, there is an emerging Afghan army, the country is getting military assistance from NATO, it has a new constitution and is holding elections, and 1.5 million refugees have opted to return and build a life. What's so wrong with that?

ROUND 7 – MICHAEL'S MADCAP MATH
BUSH IS ALWAYS TAKING LAZY VACATIONS

Michael picked up on an article in a circus magazine that claimed Bush was on vacation for 42% of his first eight months in office. Hmm. Is this the same Bush who spends every waking minute invading sovereign nations and enriching his cronies? Is there a contradiction here? Of course there is – but if Michael can keep audiences laughing, he figures nobody will care.

Naturally, quite a few people looked into this anomalous claim. Turns out that 42% figure includes weekends, which Michael failed to mention, and few presidents ever get weekends off. Turns out that 42% figure includes time spent at Camp David. Since Eisenhower, Presidents have spent many weekends at Camp David, and they conduct business there. Once the Camp David time is excluded, Bush's "vacation" time drops to 13% -- still a lot, presumably, unless you look at what a president does on a typical day while relaxing at his ranch. See the following page for a sample week from August.

With thanks to Brian Fairrington, Cagle Cartoons

President Bush Schedule During Vacation Week
(Source: www.whitehouse.gov)

Monday, August 20
- Spoke concerning the budget while visiting a high school in Independence, Missouri.
- Spoke at the annual Veteran's of Foreign Wars convention in Milwaukee, Wisconsin.
- Signed six bills into law.
- Announced 7 presidential nominees
- Spoke with workers at the Harley Davidson factory.
- Dined with Kansas Governor Bill Graves, discussing politics.

Tuesday, August 21
- Took press questions at a Target store in Kansas City, Missouri.
- Spoke with Canadian Prime Minister Jean Chretien on the matter of free trade

Wednesday, August 22
- Met with Karen Hughes, Condi Rice, and Josh Bolten, and other staff
- Conferenced with Mexico's president for on Argentina's economy and IMF role
- Communicated with Margaret LaMontagne on immigration policy meetings.
- Released the Mid-Session Review, a summary of the economic outlook for the next decade, as well as of the contemporary economy and budget.
- Announced 14 nomination and appointment intentions
- Issued a Presidential Determination ordering a military drawdown for Tunisia.
- Issued a statement regarding the retirement of Jesse Helms.

Thursday, August 23
- Briefly spoke with the press.
- Visited Crawford Elementary School, fielded questions from students.

Friday, August 24
- Officials arrived from Washington at 10:00 AM.
- At a press conference, Bush announced the Chairman of the Joint Chiefs and 15 other appointments, and his intentions for the budget.
- Met with National Security and Defense officials on the strategic review process for military transformation
- Met with Andy Card and Karen Hughes, talking about communications issues.
- Issued a proclamation honoring Women's Equality Day.

Saturday, August 25
- Received a CIA and national security briefing
- Gave weekly radio address on the topic of The Budget.

Sunday, August 26
- Speaks at the Little League World Series in Williamsport, Pennsylvania.
- Speaks at the U.S. Steel Group Steelworkers Picnic at Mon Valley Works

ROUND 8 – MICHAEL'S DOCTORED FILM
BUSH WAS FROZEN AND USELESS ON 9/11

Michael said the President looked like a deer in headlights upon hearing that the second plane had hit the World Trade Tower. It's a mean-spirited attack, and it has no basis in reality. Turns out Michael doctored the film to make Bush look so bad. When you see the same footage in *FahrenHYPE 9/11*, with narration from the school principal who was there that day in that classroom with the President, you come away with an entirely different perspective.

President Bush told the 9/11 Commission that his instinct was to project calm, not to have the country see an excited reaction in a moment of crisis. Given how terrified we all were at the moment, his instinct may have been right. Had he leapt to his feet in a take-charge stance, he probably would have been criticized as impetuous and warmongering. But and I think importantly, the guy sitting there appeared to be transformed before our eyes. Previous to 9/11, Mr. Bush was considered a lightweight – fair or not, that's how he came across to a lot of people. But 9/11 did something to Mr. Bush. We were all stunned at the growth in the man. People were talking about him differently, how he'd grown before our eyes and assumed the mantle of leadership.

We witnessed the transformation completed in his measured response to Afghanistan. Osama and his thugs were trash-talking the U.S., defying us to come after them, taunting. But Mr. Bush sat back, calm, saying he'd respond in due time. His composure under fire may have saved soldiers' lives. So it's fair to say that in those five minutes in that classroom on 9/11, Mr. Bush was pondering the mantle now upon his shoulders. He didn't react, he responded. Didn't jump for the red phone, he went inward. Maybe he was taking time to quiet his mind, to get clear. Maybe he should have been out of there in three minutes, or four. That's all conjecture. What's clear is that those few minutes transformed him for all that lay ahead.

It's interesting to inquire as to what another politician was doing that day. John Kerry was later asked by Larry King where he was on 9/11?

Kerry replied "I was in the Capitol. We'd just had a meeting - we'd just come into a leadership meeting in Tom Daschle's office, looking out at the Capitol. And as I came in, Barbara Boxer and Harry Reid were standing there, and we watched the second plane come in to the building. And we shortly thereafter sat down at the table and then we just realized nobody could think, and then boom, right behind us, we saw the cloud of explosion at the Pentagon."

The second plane hit the World Trade Center at 9:03 a.m., and the plane hit the Pentagon at 9:43 a.m. By Kerry's own words, he and his fellow senators sat there for forty minutes, realizing "nobody could think." John Kerry couldn't think for 40 minutes. George Bush took five minutes to think about it, then he declared war on terror. If the man wants to take five minutes before making such an important decision, fine!

ROUND 9 – MICHAEL'S DELIRIOUS DELUSIONS
BUSH STOLE THE FLORIDA ELECTION

In *Fahrenheit 9/11*, Michael Moore suggests that if the ballots had been recounted in the Florida election in 2000, under every scenario Gore won the election. Moore doesn't bother to share a six-month study in 2001 by *The New York Times*, the *Washington Post* and CNN – they found exactly the opposite. They concluded that if the Supreme Court had not stopped the recount, Bush still would have won Florida and the election.

And for those of you who love a conspiracy theory – are you listening, Michael? – here's a doozy. The networks – NBC, CBS and even FOX – tried to steal the election for Gore! NBC announced Gore the victor in Florida – and announced it a full 10 minutes before the polls closed in the conservative panhandle of the state. Seconds later CBS called the election for Gore. A couple minutes later Fox called it for Gore. These premature calls discouraged a lot of conservatives from voting. Were the networks in collusion with the Gore campaign? You be the judge.

We could take this refutation to all 15 rounds, but it's uncertain whether Michael could rise up out of his corner to finish the fight. He has taken too many sharp blows. He deserves to be retired a rich but morally broken man.

CHAPTER 2

ABOUT OUR
FEATURED GUESTS

 DICK MORRIS is the narrator of *FahrenHYPE 9/11*. He is a political consultant who has advised both Democrats and Republicans. For 25 years he has been the political advisor to Bill Clinton and helped formulate policy in the White House. He also advised Senate Majority Leader Trent Lott. His many bestselling books include *Rewriting History; Power Plays: Win or Lose; Off With Their Heads; The New Prince; Behind the Oval Office.* And his new book, due in October, is *Because He Could.*

 ZELL MILLER is the Democratic Senator from Georgia, following two terms as one of the nation's most popular governors. Though he is a lifelong Democrat, Miller believes his party has lost its way and explained why in the best-selling book, *A National Party No More: The Conscience of a Conservative Democrat.* Miller delivered the keynote address at the Republican National Convention, and is supporting Bush for reelection.

ED KOCH served as the 105th Mayor of New York City for three terms from 1978 to 1989, having previously served as a Congressman and member of the New York City Council. A lawyer, columnist, radio personality and partner in a law firm, Koch is a lifelong Democrat who speaks for New Yorkers and Americans everywhere when he blasts Michael Moore.

RON SILVER is an accomplished actor with over 100 stage, film and TV credits, including *The West Wing*. A liberal activist, he believes that after 9/11 we must put national security before ideology.

STEVE EMERSON is America's leading terrorism and national security expert, and serves as the Executive Director of *The Investigative Project*. Emerson wrote the best-selling *American Jihad* after creating an award-winning documentary film exposing the clandestine operations of Islamic terrorists operating on American soil.

PETER KING is a six-term Republican Congressman from New York and saw hundreds of his constituents perish on September 11th. He has been a tireless campaigner for a stronger and more vital system of homeland security. First elected in 1992, King serves on the International Relations Committee for strengthening our national defense.

ANN COULTER is the author of three best sellers — *Treason: Liberal Treachery From the Cold War to the War on Terrorism; Slander: Liberal Lies About the American Right; and High Crimes and Misdemeanors: The Case Against Bill Clinton.* Coulter is a New York attorney and has worked for the Senate Judiciary Committee, and the Center For Individual Rights.

DAVID FRUM was a speechwriter for President Bush and has published several bestselling books, including *THE RIGHT MAN: The Surprise Presidency of George W. Bush* and *AN END TO EVIL: How to Win the War on Terror.* A panelist on NPR's "Left, Right, and Center", the Wall Street Journal called Frum one of the leading political commentators of his generation.

FRANK GAFFNEY heads the Center for Security Policy, and was Reagan's Assistant Secretary of Defense. Gaffney was among the first to write that "the international situation bequeathed by Bill Clinton to George Bush was considerably more threatening than was widely perceived at the time."

DAVE KOPEL is an editor of the National Review and has written on numerous subjects, including his *59 Deceits* that chronicled the many ways Michael Moore twisted facts while masquerading as a truth-seeking documentarian. He also directs the Independence Institute, a free market think tank.

BILL SAMMON is Senior White House Correspondent for the *Washington Times*, a political analyst for the Fox News Channel, and the author most recently of *Misunderestimated: The President Battles Terrorism, John Kerry, and the Bush Haters.* He was at the Sarasota school with the President on 9/11, and offers a truthful account of the day's events.

SGT. PETER DAMON – injured in Iraq and mischaracterized in Moore's film as disillusioned and abandoned. In our film, Damon sets the record straight for himself and soldiers everywhere.

DAVID HARDY & JASON CLARKE co-authored *Michael Moore Is A Big Fat Stupid White Man* to expose how Michael Moore used facts to create fiction. Hardy is a lawyer who served for ten years with the Department of the Interior in Washington, D.C. Clarke is a web developer and outspoken critic of Michael Moore.

GWEN TOSE-RIGELL – the principal of the school Bush spoke at on 9/11 – she's a committed Gore Democrat who saw the events of that day very differently from Moore.

CHAPTER 3

BEHIND THE SCENES WITH AMERICA'S LEADING OPINION MAKERS

WE interviewed a great many Americans in the making of *FahrenHYPE 9/11*, from people who have advised presidents to people who defended our nation in combat. We have chosen some of the most poignant and insightful interviews, and reprinted them in abridged fashion here.

DICK MORRIS

(While driving across Manhattan on the way to the Brooklyn Bridge)

We're passing the United Nations building, which was one of the major terrorist targets. That was one of the first things that they singled out. And that attack was thwarted because of the very aggressive actions of the United States intelligence community. When you say there's no terrorist threat, like Michael Moore does, you just have a look at that United Nations.

We're passing here a helicopter pad. It was a result of our troops in Pakistan that we unearthed the fact that the terrorists were planning to use

these helicopters, these very ones that take tourists on trips around the skyline in Manhattan, as replacements for the jets that they used on 9/11. It is
those helicopters that during the Republican convention could have been
used for terrorist threats, but were averted because we worked with
Pakistan. Our troops went in there together, they arrested the guys, and
they went on their computers – they weren't barred from it this time
because the Patriot Act enabled them to do it – and they found that the helicopters were going to be a source of possible terrorist operations.

Standing outside the famous River Café gazing across the river at New
York City, I look at the two imaginary towers that are no longer here, the
World Trade Center towers. I see them in my mind's eye. Then I let my
glance linger just a little bit past the other buildings, all the way to the
Statue of Liberty right there. In that hole where the towers had been there
is great loss. And there in the Statue of Liberty is great hope. We're looking at what was preserved on 9/11.

The idea of liberty was preserved, the idea of freedom. That's what they
were trying to strike at, and that is still holding itself proudly aloft in the
harbor of New York City.

Brooklyn and Manhattan used to be separate cities, and they joined in
1898 and became the current city of New York because the Brooklyn
Bridge was completed. If you look under it you notice the distinct web-
bing in its cables. It was the first large bridge in the world. An engineering triumph of such magnitude that people used to say, If we can build the
Brooklyn Bridge, surely we can build the Panama Canal, or conquer yellow
fever, and so on.

This bridge was targeted by Al Qaida. Here's what happened: the CIA
picked up intercepts where people talking in Arabic kept using the word
"Brooklyn Bridge." So the CIA did something they never would have done
before the Patriot Act was passed. They said we don't care about protecting sources, we don't care about agency security or any of your bureaucrat-
ic gobbledygook. If you get information about a terrorist threat, it is a
crime not to share it with the agencies that can do something. So the CIA

With thanks to RJ Matson, Artizans

called NYPD which flooded the bridge with cops, all up and down its span, manning it all the way, continuous patrols. There are 36,000 police officers in New York City, and a lot of them were on that bridge.

And they hired an engineering firm to make a study of how to knock down this bridge. The engineering firm said you'd have to do it in a concealed location, you'd have to be able to work there for the better part of the day, and here's where you need to stand. And here's what you need to blow to make this whole thing come down. We subsequently found that was exactly what Al Qaida was planning on doing.

So anyway, this guy named Faris who was their operative, came and cased the bridge, and we picked up his signal sent back to Al Qaida saying, "the weather in New York is too hot," too hot for us to proceed with the plans. And one of the guys we captured in Pakistan and Afghanistan was Kalid Mohammad. We captured him – Moore would not have liked us to capture him. We interrogated him – Michael would have objected to that. He didn't have his attorney present, even though he was neither an American citizen nor a resident. His only connection was he was plotting to kill us, but Michael would have objected to that. And as a result of our interrogation, Kalid Mohammed told us of the plot to blow up the bridge, and he fingered Faris as the guy who was going do it.

Now before the Patriot Act, the situation would have worked out very differently. Because we would have to go to a judge and swear out a warrant. And the first question the judge would say is, What is this guy planning to do? And we'd have to say, We think he's planning to blow up the Brooklyn Bridge. And the judge would say, Okay, when is he planning to do it? And we would say, We don't know. How is he planning to do it? We don't know. Now normally when a murder's taken place you have the answers to these questions: there's the body, the murder occurred on a certain date, it was by gunshot; give us a search warrant for this guy's apartment. But before the Patriot Act we couldn't get the search warrant. Now we got the warrant, we busted the guy, we got into the apartment, we found all the surveillance tapes of the bridge. We found the engineering plans of how he was planning to blow up the bridge, and we nipped it in the bud.

Now this was not just a plan to blow up the Brooklyn Bridge. At the far end of that bridge, you see NYPD headquarters. That would have been demolished in an attack on the Brooklyn Bridge. The entire command structure of the whole New York City Police Department, from the commissioner on down, would have been obliterated if that building went. And right nearby as well is City Hall. The mayor would have been killed, and the entire city government. Also nearby is the Municipal Building, where all of the city workers are. And nearby is the federal courthouse -- that also would have been destroyed.

When Michael Moore says there's no terrorist threat, I'd like to meet him in the middle of the Brooklyn Bridge and talk about it.

There was another plot thwarted because of our capture and interrogation under the Patriot Act of Kalid Mohammad. We learned that Al Qaida had earmarked $100,000 to buy an import firm and a trucking company in the garment center in Manhattan, at about 35th Street and 7th Avenue. Their goal was to buy this company, which had a clean record, and therefore the containers they imported from Kashmir would not be searched, and they could load the container with explosives and rockets and missiles, bring it in through Newark Airport, put it on a container truck, drive it into the middle of Manhattan, and blow it up. And because we interrogated Kalid Mohammad, we stopped that operation.

And it's not just New York. There was a terrorist cell in San Diego, California that was broken up. There was a threat on LAX that was broken up. The Al Qaida operatives were seen casing the Hoover Dam to see if they could explode that. There is surveillance footage that we discovered in Spain from Al Qaida operatives of the MGM Grand Excalibur and New York New York casinos in Las Vegas, where 11,000 people live on any given day in hotel rooms. There was the terrorist cell broken up in Portland, Oregon, one in Lackawanna New York, one in northern Virginia.

The IMF Building and the World Bank in Washington were targeted. Fact is, they're targeting every one of us. This is a phenomenon that affects us all. It affects our country. And I believe that it's very important that a video come out which has the truth.

Personally, I think Michael Moore's film is a great example of our freedoms. I am so proud that I live in a country that can tolerate a film that says that it's criminal, that says that it spreads barbarism throughout the world, that undermines our motivation and knocks our troops at a time of war, and it can be at every theater in the country and it can make a lot of money, and it can be in video stores, and nobody's in jail as a result of it. So Michael Moore's film, in trying to knock our liberty, and trying to say that we don't have any, is the best illustration of how wrong his film is.

Standing here in New York on another beautiful day, I can still remember all of the feelings of 9/11 – I suppose I'll never forget. It was a beautiful day. We don't get many beautiful days in New York. Either it's too hot or too cold. This was September so it was just after a really hot, muggy, awful, terrible, humid summer. And it was cool. You could see all the way down the west side to the Statue of Liberty from my apartment on 62nd Street. And it was like you woke up and said, This is a day that the Lord made.

Now I flew in from Brazil and landed at Kennedy Airport at 6:30 in the morning. And as the cab took me in over the bridges into Manhattan, I looked at the Trade Center as part of the skyline – I always thrilled to that view. By the time I got through customs it was 8:00. And the plane hit it around 8:30 I think – it was like somebody took the most beautiful, gorgeous painting you've ever seen and just threw mud on it.

You had to actually be in New York for 9/11 for the sickening sound of the bodies hitting to truly understand. I was not at Ground Zero, I was 4 miles away so I didn't hear it. But then when I heard the tapes of 9/11, that sound – and you just – it's a sound you've never heard before, of just fwap. And I've spoken to reporters who were there, who really had to take a year or two off, they just couldn't handle it.

And I remember immediately after the attacks – I live about 4 blocks from the Red Cross Headquarters. And my wife and friends walked to the

With thanks to Linda Eddy, Iowa Presidential Watch

Red Cross building and we lined up outside to give blood, and there were hundreds of people lined up outside to give blood. And then it just became apparent that nobody needed any blood that day, they were all dead. And incredibly, all of the people in our office, a company called vote.com, started walking north. And everybody was walking north. Everybody was walking uptown. And not a word, not a horn honk, not a beep, nobody talking. Just total silence. And then when we got to about 50th Street, Rockefeller Center, a plane flew overhead. And everybody tensed, everybody just froze. They all looked up. And it turned out it was one of ours, it was not another hijacked plane, it was a military jet.

And then when we learned that the military was flying jets 24 hours over the city, and we learned about all of the help that New York was getting, we had this feeling of being protected, being loved by the country, being protected.

And then there was that moment that just so chokes you up. They're interviewing the fire commissioner. And they asked about the firemen running into the building as it was collapsing. And the reporter asked, Are you gonna get any of the firemen out? And he said, Firefighters run into buildings, we don't run out of them.

I think that the dominant thing that the White House people were probably feeling is that they were present at a fundamental departure in our history. You can't be in the White House without having the sense that you're actually in the pages of a history book. But this was more. You become instantly conscious that this was the day the bomb was dropped in Hiroshima, this was the day of Pearl Harbor, this was the day Fort Sumter was fired on, this was the day of Appomattox, this was the day of the victory at Yorktown, this was the day of the Declaration of Independence being signed, this was the day the Mayflower landed. This is one of those seminal moments in our history.

When something horrible happens, when there's a disaster or major threat, the security apparatus respond in their own way, and they have all of their command communications and their logistics. And it's very impressive, and I don't really know each of the things that happen. But I do know what goes on in the mind of a president of the United States when he gets cataclysmic, horrible news. And you have to realize that the President of the United States lives in one of two states of being: on camera or off camera. Indoors, outdoors, Washington, outside, foreign, domestic, with his family, with his advisors, with foreign dignitaries, doesn't matter. It's either on camera or it's off camera. And a president understands that his first obligation when he's on camera is to be on camera, that at that point he is as much a symbol of the United States of America as the flag is.

And I think that when Bush is criticized for those 7 minutes, those were on camera minutes. Listen, if 9/11 happened and Bush were in the Oval Office and he were alone and not on camera, and Card walked in a gave him a note and said that another plane hit the towers, America's under attack, and he sat in his chair in the Oval Office staring into the distance for 7 minutes, get that man out of there. But on camera, under-reacting, not panicking, reassuring the country by his presence, by his stability, not causing mass panic – I really understand that.

Look I don't understand why people hate Bush. I just don't get it. In fact I've been reading a lot of books lately to try to give me a handle on it, because I'm supposed to be a political analyst, and it's not good if you don't understand what's going on. Me, I feel sheltered, protected and all that by him, because I'm a New Yorker.

Before he was elected, I thought, Gee I don't want another son of a famous father, I don't want a guy whose life experience started when he was 40 and he stopped drinking, I don't want a guy who never had to work cause he had a golden foot in his mouth. So I voted for Gore in 2000. But when I saw him step up after 9/11 – and I had been urging Clinton to do just that – at that moment he became my president. And I'll tell you my attitude toward him. On September 11th they were shooting at me. You know, in Catch 22 he says, Somebody's trying to kill me. And they say, How do you know? And he says, Somebody's shooting at me. And they say, What does that matter, they're shooting at everybody. And he says,

What difference does that make? And so as a New Yorker I felt they were shooting at me. And when you're getting shot at, you're in the army, whether you know it or not, and in the army you follow your commander in chief and you try to make his job easier.

And it isn't just 9/11. Every two weeks we'd have to vacate the office, there'd be a threat. And everybody would silently pad down 17 flights of stairs to evacuate the building, and we'd all stand out there with the smokers. We were all out there on the sidewalk, and you just don't say anything, you just look at each other. It's like you're in a sub and you don't want to say anything cause you don't want the torpedo to hit you, and you think that if you talk or something, it'll draw attention. I mean t's that constant, constant fear. And that's not fabricated fear, that's not manufactured fear. That's real, serious fear.

I live 62 miles from Ground Zero. The effective radius of a nuclear bomb is about 40 miles of deadly radiation and of the initial shock. I know that fact, I've thought about that fact, and I live 20 miles past that, and I thank my stars every day for those 20 miles. You know, I'm not nuts. It's the guys that don't understand that that are nuts.

Michael Moore can say anything he wants to say. I'm not saying the guy's a traitor, I'm not saying he's anti-patriotic, I'm not saying he's anti-American; he's not. Everybody has the right to say anything they bloody well want. They have the right to put it on the movie, they have a right to put it out there, and if you don't want it, don't watch it, and don't buy it. And I don't believe in any form of censorship at all, I just don't care. You let him do whatever he wants to do. But that doesn't mean we can't answer it. That doesn't mean we can't rebut it. You know the first amendment applies to us too.

Somebody has to tell the country the truth about terrorists. Somebody has to explain to the country its importance. And someone has to explain that nobody took it seriously before George Bush on 9/11. Bush gets eight months of blame, Clinton had eight years of blame.

Bush is now taking it seriously. That's the reason this country is safe.

And somebody has to point that out. It can't be somebody in the administration, because you figure that's what they're getting paid to say. And it can't be one of the usual right wing, because they're going to line up for Bush no matter. It's got to be somebody that may have some credibility. And that's why we made this movie with so many credible, courageous Americans.

If people take nothing else from this film, they must get that George Bush kept us safe for 3 years. If I told you on September 12th, 2001, there would not be another major terrorist hit in the United States for three years, you would have said I was nuts. People were wondering, would it be next week, would it be next month.

Everybody thought anthrax might have been Al Qaida, everybody was flipping out about it.

And it wasn't that they didn't try. We're sitting here at this studio at 51st Street and Lexington Avenue, and 8 blocks up that way is the Citicorp Center, which they were casing. And 40 blocks down that way is the New York City Stock Exchange they were casing. And 45 blocks that way is the Brooklyn Bridge that a guy actually tried to knock down and blow up. And 12 blocks that way is the garment center where they tried to take over this garment company so they could bring a truckload full of explosives off a ship container into midtown Manhattan and blow the place to smithereens. So when people ask me, When do you think Al Qaida will hit us?, my answer is, They're gonna keep trying, but George Bush is continuing to stop 'em. And hey, I don't always like the guy, I don't agree with him on a whole lot of things. I voted for Gore in 2000. But this guy kept us safe, and he's entitled to get some slack cut for that.

Our film, *FahrenHYPE 9/11* is the antidote. I mean, if you're going to swallow something with a skull and crossbones on it, take an antidote. Michael says we're not facing a terrorist threat. He said that's the biggest lie we're being told. Yeah Michael, tell me about it. He said 9/11 was people making too much of a big deal out of 9/11. Yeah, you tell me about that.

He said that Bush has done nothing and was comatose after 9/11. Yeah, you tell me about that. Somebody's got to set the record straight, and that's what this film is all about.

Bill Clinton and I had a wonderful collaboration on every issue except one – terror. In fact in August of 1996, right after Clinton signed the Welfare Reform Bill, we had this conversation where we talked about his place in history. And he said, What would I have to do to move up in my place in history? And I said three things: sign the Welfare Reform Bill and make it work, balance the federal budget, and break the back of international terrorism by military and economic means. I wrote about this in my 1997 book *Behind the Oval Office*. And he just didn't get the terror thing. You know, Meatloaf has this song: 2 Out of 3 Ain't Bad. Well, two out of three wasn't enough for the country.

It all goes back to what happened right after he was elected. Thirty days after he took the oath of office, Al Qaida bombed the World Trade Center with the goal of toppling the thing. They wanted to kill a quarter of a million people, and their idea was to topple one building into the other. They exploded a bomb in the parking garage, wiped out six stories, killed six people, hospitalized a thousand. And Clinton was just preoccupied. That was roughly the same day the Waco siege began, Branch Davidian. It was right at the height of the gays and the military controversy. It was right when he was trying to get his economic stimulus package through.

Clinton never visited the trade center, never took it seriously. Even in his memoirs, *My Life*, he devotes only one paragraph to that 1993 bombing. But in retrospect, that was the first foreign attack on American soil since the British burned Washington in the War of 1812. And it really was the tip-off. But instead of taking that investigation and making a national crisis out of it, using it aggressively to mobilize the country, he just said, "Don't overreact." That's a quote.

So the investigation of the bombing was slow tracked. Instead of the FBI and CIA and all the national security types running it, they had the U.S. Attorney for the Southern District of New York running it, just like it was a bank robbery or a kidnapping or a homicide. And the result was that it wasn't until five years later that bin Laden was indicted.

As the '90s progressed, Clinton began to realize that this terror threat wasn't going away. You had the bombing of the U.S.S. Cole, you had the bombing of our embassies in Africa, you had the bombing of Kobar Towers where our troops were stationed in Saudi Arabia. So gradually it got higher and higher profile. But the curve of raising attention never matched the curve you had to go of actual action. So we were always one or two steps behind.

For example, in 1996, bin Laden was in the Sudan. He'd been there for 4 or 5 years. And the Sudanese were on our terror list, and they wanted to get off. They said, We want to come in from the cold, we don't want you to post sanctions on us. So they said, We've got Osama bin Laden in our country and we want to throw him out. Do you want him? Now the defense minister of the Sudan says he actually offered bin Laden to the United States. The 9/11 Commission says they can't completely confirm that. But it is clear that Sudan asked bin Laden to leave. So they next asked where they should send him? At that point the U.S. could have said, To us! But we didn't. We said, Why don't you send him to Saudi Arabia. And the Saudis said, We don't want anything to do with this guy. We know he's a Saudi national, but he's bad news, we don't want him in our country. So he went to Afghanistan instead.

So why didn't we take him when we could? Because we didn't have any reason to hold him, he hadn't committed a crime. He'd bombed the World Trade Center, and he'd committed lots of crimes against the American people, but we hadn't proven it, cause that investigation was a mule train. So by the time the mule train arrived at an answer, bin Laden was in the mountains of Afghanistan under a friendly regime and there was no way we could find him.

Then in 1997, the CIA gets its act together and says, We're going after bin Laden. And they develop this really good plan that the 9/11 Commission says was the most sophisticated ever, to work with the local

With thanks to Steve Kelley, Cartoonist Group

Afghanistan tribes that hated bin Laden. They would kidnap him, they'd fly him to the middle of the desert, they'd hold him there, and then the U.S. would come in, snatch him and bring him to the United States. They even had a dress rehearsal, a dry run. Everything was all set to go. And then Sandy Berger, the National Security Advisor, and George Tenet, the head of the CIA, vetoed it. And do you know why? They were afraid bin Laden would be hurt. They were afraid that in the course of kidnapping him, he might get killed, he might get shot. And why were they worried about that? Because the President of the United States had not signed what's called a memorandum of notification, giving the CIA the authority to use lethal force to apprehend bin Laden or to kill him. And why hadn't he signed it yet? Because the investigation was slow tracked. This is all in the 9/11 commission report. We were afraid bin Laden might be hurt!

Then in 1998, the CIA came up with a better idea. They said, Okay we're not allowed to assassinate bin Laden, but if he dies in an air strike, that's okay. So they got intelligence as to where bin Laden was going to be. Clinton got up his gumption, and we fired 20 or 30 cruise missiles. They go low over the ocean, they go over Pakistan, they go into Afghanistan and they hit bin Laden – where we think bin Laden is. And it turns out the son of a gun left an hour or two before our missiles hit. Why? Because some genius in the administration said, We have to tip off the Pakistanis that we're going to do this raid, because we're going to overfly their air space, and they might think these missiles are from India, and we'll start a nuclear war.

Everybody knew that Pakistan was a sieve, that if you tell the Pakis they were going to tell bin Laden. Nonetheless, we sent over the Army Deputy Chief of Staff. He met with the head of the Pakistani army, and told him about the raid. And somehow bin Laden got tipped off and left two hours before.

Then, the rest of the country went ballistic. They yelled, "Wag the dog!" And this was all happening two days after Clinton's grand jury testimony on Monica Lewinsky. And everyone is claiming he did this just to distract attention from his grand jury testimony.

The result of all this was, when again in 1999 we had even better evidence as to where bin Laden was going to be and we knew we could take him out, Clinton pulled the plug because he worried people would yell, "wag the dog." So whether it's the Republicans raising hell, or whether it was Clinton's timidity, we basically let the guy go.

We wouldn't even bribe to get him. At one point we came up with a plan to pay the Taliban a quarter of a billion dollars to turn over bin Laden to us. They could have done it. Richard Clark, the guy who wrote Against All Enemies, the anti-terror guy who's dumping on Bush, killed the bribe plan because he said that we couldn't be seen paying money to an anti-feminist regime like the Taliban, that Hillary Clinton and Madeleine Albright would raise hell. I'm not making this stuff up! It's actually in the 9/11 Commission Report!

We let opportunity after opportunity after opportunity to get this guy just slip through our fingers. In fact, when that 1999 air raid was canceled, the guys who were running it slumped in their chair and buried their head in their hands and said, If this intelligence isn't good enough for us to act on, nothing ever will be.

So why did Clinton do this? I mean, was he dumb? He's not dumb. It was that nobody understood what 9/11 could be. Nobody really understood the importance of getting bin Laden. Clinton's head was still back in Vietnam and Bay of Pigs, and the failed hostage rescue mission, and the Lebanon barracks. And the only thing that could happen in a military action, to his way of thinking, was that you could screw it up.

Indeed, the last time there had been a military action on Clinton's watch, it was screwed up. In Mogadishu 19 American servicemen were killed and they dragged the body of one of the soldiers through the streets. And Clinton didn't respond aggressively, he just said, Let's get out of there, let's pull out. I spoke to Hillary Clinton by phone, and she said, This is Bush's welcome to the White House present -- we got to get out of there. But you know who was watching? Osama bin Laden. In 1999 he gave an interview to Esquire magazine where he actually said, I was watching Mogadishu. I saw the Americans pull out, and I realized the United States was a paper tiger. So when we appeased people like we did in Somalia, it backfired.

You know, we give Bush all kinds of negative rap because 9/11 happened on his watch, and okay the guy deserves 8 months of blame. But Clinton deserves 8 years of blame. And you know, when you come into the White House it takes a while to find out where the bathroom is, it takes a couple of months to get up to speed. And to change these policies – it's hard to turn a battleship around.

But the big failure of the Clinton administration was not only not in getting bin Laden, it was in not making the air system safe. We had lots of crashes, lots of hijackings. We had the TWA 800 flight that people thought was terrorism. We had the Lockerbie crash, which was terrorism. We knew the terrorists were targeting airplanes.

I was working with Clinton at the time. I said, Hey you've – this issue is going to kill us if we don't get ahead of it. So Clinton appointed Gore to head a commission on air safety procedures. And the Gore commission set up CAPPS -- Civil Aviation Passenger Pre-Screening System. This was a system where they developed a mathematical formula, an algorithm (an Al-Gore-rithm!) designed to predict who could be a hijacker, who could be a saboteur. It worked!

Of the 19 hijackers on 9/11, the system fingered eight of them, pulled them out for special scrutiny. But you know what? They changed the rules so that the only thing we would do when we fingered someone who's a risk, was make sure their baggage got on the plane with them, because we assumed that nobody would ever commit suicide in a hijacking.

And the result is that when CAPPS tagged Mohammad Atta and the other terrorists, there was no extra search, no second run through the metal detector, no patting them down, no interrogating them, authorities just held them until the bags were on the plane, and then they made sure they

With thanks to Linda Eddy, Iowa Presidential Watch

got on the plane. We had those terrorists in our grasp!

And by the way, when we searched them we found a box cutter with a big blade on a four inch knife and a can of mace or pepper spray – the weapons they actually used. We let them get on the plane with those weapons because those weapons were expressly permitted by a 1994 ruling of the FAA, on Clinton's watch, which said that we have to allow these in. Why? Because civilians were allowed to carry them on the street. And why should they be tougher in air traffic?

Did it take an active imagination to think that you could kill somebody with a 4 inch knife, or that you could put a box cutter to a flight attendant's neck, which is just what those guys did?

So you can say, How did Clinton know about bin Laden, how did he know about 9/11? But he knew that an aircraft could be very, very dangerous. And then he goes before the Democratic convention and he says, We are going to search every plane and every cargo hold every time. I know those lines because I wrote it for him in a speech. It was this big deal that he gave. But it was total nonsense, it was total garbage. Nothing ultimately happened.

One day I met with Clinton and I said, "Hey, what is the major way that we come in contact with cops, with the police establishment? Traffic cops, okay? I know, because I have a lot of experience with those guys! Half of all people here illegally come in legally on a visa, and then they overstay their visa. And we really do not have a system for finding those people. So I said, Let's make drivers licenses expire when visas do for immigrants, so that if a cop pulls somebody over and sees that they don't have a license, he can check in a database on his computer, interface it with the INS and the FBI and see if this guy's here illegally, and if he's a wanted terrorist. And then if he is, you grab him right then and then arrange for deportation.

Clinton rejected this idea because George Stephanopoulos, his communications director, said it would hurt the Hispanic base. What, Hispanics like hijackers?

So when a cop pulled over Mohammad Atta, a little over 4 months before 9/11 in Florida and found he didn't have a valid drivers license, the cop went back to the computer, typed it in, saw there were no other traffic violations, and gave Atta a summons. He never showed up in court and he slipped through our fingers. Two other hijackers were also arrested for speeding, and we just didn't follow up. They were all here illegally. We could have run them out of the country. bin Laden could have been dead. There could have been an effective air traffic control system. But there wasn't.

In his movie, Michael Moore mocks all of the efforts to make our country safer. He wouldn't be mocking so much if any of those terrorists operations had succeeded. But fortunately for our nation Bush has gone after these terrorist cells one by one and broken them up. He's done it with incredibly intensive surveillance, incredibly intensive interrogations, and the inter-agency cooperation that the Patriot Act requires.

So take all of the facts, take the information we're presenting here, add them up any way you want: vote for Bush, vote for Kerry, stay undecided. But know the facts. That's what this is about.

ED KOCH

DICK MORRIS: Mayor Koch, what was it was like to be a New Yorker on 9/11?

MAYOR KOCH: It was overwhelming. I was in my law office, and my secretary came running in and said, "We just heard there's a report of an accidental plane crash, small plane; let's turn on the TV." We did. First there was nothing, because the cables were down. And then it came back on. And we saw initially the first hit. And suddenly live of the second hit. People were crying. I live at lower 5th Avenue, and I would say it's about a mile and a half from point zero. And you could smell death in the air for months. It's that sweet smell that comes when flesh is mortifying. It was awful. And then everybody else knows somebody who was killed.

MORRIS: I felt like I had teeth extracted. You know, I was born in New York City, and lived here my whole life, went to school here. And I feel like, I had 2 molars in the back of my mouth that were pulled. And whenever I see the skyline, unconsciously my tongue goes to that spot to make sure my teeth are all still there.

KOCH: It was all brought home to me when there were services a year later and I was asked to read some of the names of the dead. And I was sitting next to the father of one of the young women who was killed. He was from Wisconsin. He saw it all happening. He was called on the phone by neighbors, and his daughter was in that building at that particular moment, and as he related it to me, I began to weep. It was just awful. On occasion, I still weep when I think about it.

MORRIS: I feel very much that my city was exposed and endangered, and left naked to terrorism. And now when I look at the terror plots on the sub-

'The Thinker'
1880

'The Tinker'
2004

With thanks to Juju Dandridge Suits

ways, on the Brooklyn Bridge, on the stock exchange, on the Citicorp Center, the Newark airport, and I look at how one after another they've been foiled under this administration, I have a feeling of being protected.

KOCH: I believe that they're doing a good job, but there's a lot more that has to be done. There's no question that the examination of the container ships is not yet adequate. But they're getting there. I've never voted for a Republican president. I think of myself as a good Democrat. And I tried to bring the party closer to the center, because I'm a centrist myself.

I describe myself as a liberal with sanity. And I think it's a description that most Democrats would apply to themselves. But regrettably, the party is oftentimes taken over by the radicals on the left, the McGovern people, the Dean people. And you have to stand up and fight 'em. And I have decided that's exactly what I'm going to do. Because we're at war! And these people want to kill us. That's not my statement, that's Lee Hamilton, who is the deputy chairman of the 9/11 Commission, he said, "These people want to kill us." And who is he talking about? He's talking about the Islamic fundamentalists. They're not a majority, but they are an ever-growing minority. And because there are over a billion Muslims, that there are many millions who are supporters of bin Laden. They believe that if Christians and Jews and Hindus and other religions don't accept the supremacy of Islam, they are to be killed. And well, I'd rather kill them, and I'd rather it be done in other countries before they come here.

I get very upset with the people who denounce the Patriot Act. I ask them a question, I say: "Do you know what's in the Patriot Act?" Well they'll mumble, and then I'll say, "Can you tell me one thing that the Patriot Act does that you don't like?" And invariably most of them can't. The fact is that Diane Feinstein, the liberal Democratic senator from California, said she had asked the American Civil Liberties Union for one case where someone's rights had been taken away as a result of the use of the Patriot Act. And the American Civil Liberties Union said to her, "We don't have a single case."

MORRIS: There's a heartbreaking story about the chance we had to break up the 9/11 plot a month before it happened. FBI agents in Minnesota noticed that Zacharias Mussawi, the 20th hijacker, was attending flight school. He didn't want to know how to land or take off, he just wanted to know how to steer an airplane. So it was suspicious, and they checked the INS records and they found that he was here illegally. They arrested him, and they detained him. But the Clinton administration had set up a wall between the prosecutors of a crime and the intelligence agents trying to thwart an attack. So the FBI couldn't check the laptop computer of the illegal immigrant. It was relevant to the intelligence people, but the FBI couldn't cross the wall and they didn't open the computer.

KOCH: I believe that one of the most reprehensible things is allowing of the FBI director, Louis Freeh, and the CIA director George Tenet, to go Scott free. It happened on their watch! They deserve to be held responsible. I'm not saying that we should beat them up or put them in jail. But we should have fixed responsibility. I think our legislators failed in that respect.

MORRIS: You know, we look at the targets that Al Qaeda terrorists have aimed at in the days since 9/11, and you just are amazed that we've gotten away so far without one of them being hit. Let me ask you a question: If on September 12th I had come to you and I'd said, "there will not be another terrorist attack for 3 years," would you have believed me?

KOCH: No I wouldn't have believed you. You know, if things go wrong you blame the people in charge -- the President, his cabinet, and so forth. If things go right, they deserve the credit.

MORRIS: What has Bush done, except protect us?

KOCH: I agree. I think he is a good president. He has enunciated a rule of law which I think rivals the Monroe Doctrine and the Truman Doctrine. The Bush Doctrine is, "We will go after the terrorists, and the countries that harbor them." You think John Kerry's going to do that? I don't think so. I know his supporters don't want that.

MORRIS: When you look at the targets that these horrible Al Qaeda operatives have targeted, they roll off your tongue: the Brooklyn Bridge, the stock exchange, the Citicorp Tower. There was one incredible episode where Al Qaeda tried to buy a garment center company that imported things from Kashmir, so they could smuggle in a bomb in a truck into midtown Manhattan, a huge bomb that might have gone off in the garment center. Now you were mayor of New York. Brooklyn Bridge, right near Lower Manhattan. Stock exchange in Lower Manhattan. Citicorp Tower, dominating midtown Manhattan. The garment center, the area right between them next to all of the city's transportation facilities. What would the impact of those strikes have been?

KOCH: We would have been devastated as a city for years to come. You know, when people say to me, "can they do something that would actually bring the city to its knees?" My immediate response, because I am a New Yorker, is "No! No!" But if you have enough of these incidents, the answer obviously is "yes."

And how do you cope with that in your mind? Well, I think you have to lead your life like you led it before, more aware of who's with you, who's behind you, what the packages are that are lying there unattended, but not let it prevent you from leading your life. Otherwise, and though it sounds hackneyed to say it, otherwise the terrorists have won. If they're able to change our civilization in terms of the way we lead our lives, they've won. But we're not going to let them. We're so extraordinarily resilient. New Yorkers are very proud that we stood up. We had a mayor who excelled on that day. Nobody could have done it better. And he did it with such

By permission of John Deering and Creators Syndicate, Inc.

aplomb that he will go down in history as one of the great mayors. And he's entitled—

MORRIS: And you know he almost died on that day.

KOCH: Yes. People were killed all around him from the flying debris. And people who had been with him shortly before he entered a building, who were in the uniformed services at top levels, when he came out a few minutes later they were dead.

MORRIS: Incredible. Now how do you think Michael Moore reacted to 9/11?

KOCH: Well Michael Moore, if I may say so, is a dog. A miserable dog. And the reason - I will tell you why I came to that conclusion – I went to see his movie. But before I –

MORRIS: Are you saying that Michael Moore has all the qualities of a dog except loyalty?

KOCH: I met him shortly after 9/11. The BBC put together a round table, and they were anti-American and anti-anything decent in my judgment. But they had me and a couple of people who were supportive of America. And I remember just before they went live to Great Britain, Michael Moore was talking, and he said "You make too much of these deaths. You're more likely to be struck by lightning than an act of a terrorism." I was horrified. I said, "three thousand people were murdered, how can you say this?" It didn't bother him. Now, in addition to being a partner in a law firm, I do movie reviews. So I went to see *Fahrenheit 9/11* and I wrote that it was well done, there's no question. But, it's not a documentary. It's a lie.

I'll give you an illustration. He said that the bin Laden family was spirited out of the country by order of the president and he wondered aloud why we weren't getting that information. Turns out, it wasn't true. It was Richard Clark who ordered it. He was the terrorist expert at the White House. He hates the president, but apparently he is an honorable man, and he told the 9/11 Commission that he was the one who ordered that they be flown out, and that before they were flown out the FBI interviewed everyone they wanted to interview in that family. I think 31 people were interviewed. Michael Moore had to know that. But that didn't fit in with his story, so he didn't tell us that.

MORRIS: I can't believe when Moore says that there is no terrorist threat in the United States.

KOCH: Such a schmuck I have yet to meet.

MORRIS: When we hear somebody say there's no terrorist threat in the United States, and that there's three times greater chance of being struck by lightning than being hit by a terrorist attack, and on the way home today you we are going to drive by that huge, gigantic, ugly, miserable, horrible crater, you have to wonder about the accuracy of Mr. Moore.

KOCH: We know he doesn't care about facts. And as a result, his movie has been torn apart quite correctly. Those who go to see it who are already filled with hate, politically against Bush, they will hate more. Those who don't have those feelings will not be incited to have them.

MORRIS: One of the terrorist threats since 9/11 is just chilling. U.S. authorities intercepted a guy who had smuggled a Stinger missile into the United States and was planning to smuggle 50 more of them in. He was going to set up outside of Newark Airport and shoot an airplane as it took off. How did this intercept happen? From the interagency cooperation made possible by the Patriot Act.

KOCH: Let me talk about the Patriot Act, because the radicals and civil libertarians constantly cite the Patriot Act. I thank God we have the Patriot Act.

MORRIS: One of the provisions of the Patriot Act is something that the Clinton administration pressed for, and Congress didn't give him. That was an update in wire tap authority based on the updates in phone technology. Under the old rules, if the FBI wanted to tap you, they would get a wire tap order for you on your phone. If you used another phone, or your cell phone, it wasn't covered. So Clinton said, "why don't we just do the wiretap on the person, on anything that he or she is doing, not on the telephone?" It was rejected. But finally Bush put it into the Patriot Act.

KOCH: Right. And the leftists say, "oh, the library! They can go and check what books I've taken out." Yes, they can under a subpoena, and I would like to know if someone has taken out a book on how to build a nuclear bomb. What's wrong with that?

MORRIS: I don't think they're monitoring people who read Steinbeck, I think it's bomb manuals. And the other thing that's in the Patriot Act: In the past, we could not search or seize or wiretap anybody unless we could tell what crime they committed, when they committed it, and what we're looking for. Now that's okay for the criminal justice system – the murder happens, the body's there, he was killed by a knife, we want to go into his apartment and look at the knife for this crime on this date. But when you're trying to stop something from happening in the future, and you have no idea what this terrorist cell is going to pull off, shouldn't we be able to at least investigate whether the guy is a member of a terrorist group?

KOCH: There actually is very little chance of stopping a terrorist attack except through the infiltration of the cell, so you become privy to what it is that they're thinking.

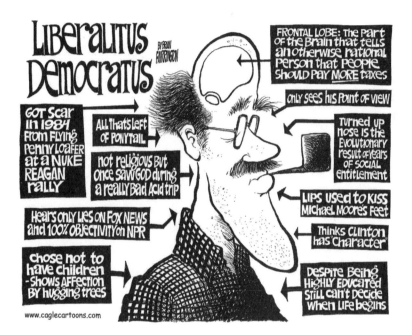

With thanks to Brian Fairrington, Cagle Cartoons

MORRIS: One of the provisions in the Patriot Act is: If I get information on you from a surveillance I conducted because you're a member of a terrorist group, with the special warrants that are issued under the act, not a warrant issued by a judge, I cannot use it to prosecute you. I cannot use it to lock you up, I can't use it to indict you, I can't use it to convict you. What I can do is use it to stop you from killing somebody else. So there's a real question as to whether we're gonna be able to convict Zacharias Mussawi, the 20th hijacker. Because the information we receive may not be usable for prosecution.

KOCH: It was Supreme Court Justice Jackson who said, "The Constitution is not a suicide pact." And that sort of sums up the feelings of most people.

MORRIS: And by the way, that was the Justice who presided at the Nuremburg trials, so he obviously had some sensitivity. A little more sensitivity than Michael Moore who said, "the Patriot Act is the first step. Mein Kampf was written long before Hitler took power, and if the people in Germany had understood what Hitler was planning in Mein Kampf, maybe we could have averted some of that."

Before you were mayor of New York, you were one of the leaders of the peace movement against the Vietnam War. You stood up very valiantly and very aggressively. So how would you compare today's peace movement with that one?

KOCH: In the Vietnamese controversy, North Vietnam, South Vietnam, my position was – a plague on both their houses. The North Vietnamese were Communists, with all the repression that comes from that. The South Vietnamese were corrupt and somewhat Fascist, with all the repression that comes from that. Why should we be there? That was my position, and I opposed the war. I have no regrets about that. This is totally different. I mean, we were attacked. We lost 3,000 people, innocent civilians who were killed by terrorists. We have to see justice done.

MORRIS: Many people would say that's why we went into Afghanistan, but Iraq didn't attack us on 9/11.

KOCH: Iraq was a threat to the region, and to us in the foreseeable future. There's no question that everybody at the U.N. was told they have biological weapons, they have chemical weapons, and they're working on nuclear weapons. They used poison gas on their own people!

MORRIS: Even Adolf Hitler didn't use poison gas on the battlefield. The Soviets didn't use poison gas in Afghanistan. We lost Vietnam rather than resort to poison gas. The only use of poison gas since 1918 in combat was Saddam Hussein against the Kurds and against the Iranians.

KOCH: Tommy Franks, commander of the forces that conquered Iraq, put out a book and he said "I thought they had chemical weapons, and I was prepared for it, and biological weapons. I was told this by the President of Egypt and the King of Saudi Arabia." So if the neighboring countries believed at that time that he had them, why shouldn't we believe it?

MORRIS: I believe there's a more basic point. I don't care what brand of terrorist we're talking about – Sunni, Shiite, Wahhabi, secular or for that matter IRA or Basque or FARC in Columbia – a terrorist is a terrorist is a terrorist. And Bush declared war on the genre.

KOCH: Yes.

MORRIS: And Saddam Hussein himself is a weapon of mass destruction.

KOCH: Saddam Hussein told the United Nations at the end of Gulf War

I in 1991 that he did have these weapons, but that he had destroyed them, but he wouldn't allow a verification. So it was absolutely responsible and reasonable to believe that Iraq had the wherewithal to threaten the region and to supply other terrorists that could threaten us.

MORRIS: Let's say that you knew back then that we would not find any weapons of mass destruction. And let's say that you knew he had destroyed all of his weapons. Do you still think that the war and the invasion of Iraq, even knowing that, was the right thing to do?

KOCH: It was absolutely the right thing to do. We had a responsibility to go in and prevent this tyrant from killing, murdering his own people, gouging out eyes, cutting off tongues. They have found more than 300,000 bodies. They expect to find a million bodies. We can't walk away from that any more. There was a time when Adolf Hitler was doing that, and people walked away. Can't do that any more. You can't do it in the Sudan, you can't do it in Rwanda, and Burundi, and you can't do it in Iraq. And so I if I were a Congressman, I would definitely have voted to declare war against Iraq, even if I knew there were no weapons of mass destruction.

MORRIS: And we know Saddam Hussein was committed to doing everything he possibly could to do as much harm to the United States as he conceivably could.

KOCH: For us, 9/11 was the equivalent of what happened at Pearl Harbor. It alerted the country.

MORRIS: Who attacked us in Pearl Harbor? The Japanese! Was Adolf Hitler responsible for Pearl Harbor? Was there a single shred of evidence that Adolf Hitler caused Pearl Harbor? Were there any meetings between the Japanese and the Germans where they plotted about Pearl Harbor? No. So by Michael Moore's definition, we should have declared war on Japan

maybe, but certainly not against Adolf Hitler. All he was doing was exterminating his own people.

I personally believe that there are 8 nations in the world that sponsor terrorism. One of them is Afghanistan, one of them is Iraq. When we went into Iraq and arrested Saddam Hussein, three weeks later Qaddafi in Libya gave up the ghost, opened up his whole country, said "come on in and look at everything, I'm dismantling my program." Do you think those were connected?

KOCH: There's no question that they were connected.

MORRIS: Some people say it was the sanctions that turned Qaddafi.

KOCH: The sanctions didn't work.

MORRIS: Well, the sanctions worked to the extent that they were willing to turn over the Lockerbie hijackers, and pay money to all the victims. But to dismantle their nuclear and their biological and chemical weapons programs? No way. And when Saddam Hussein was arrested, suddenly all that changed. I was on a BBC program the day after Saddam's arrest, and they asked me, "do I feel that the fact that Saddam was arrested with his hair crazy and without a chance to clean up, and the probing in his mouth, was an undignified treatment of him which would stimulate a backlash against him in the Arab world." I replied "these guys cut off people's hands, and what do you want, hair and makeup for a dictator?"

What do you say to people who think we should have waited for our allies before invading Iraq?

KOCH: Colin Powell deserves a lot of credit for taking every possible effort to convince the members of the Security Council to join us. But they were not convincible. Some of them had been bribed. Others like France not only bribed, but also resentful of the fact that they were no longer a nation that could be considered in the same sentence as the United States. Their past was now their present, and they simply resented us.

MORRIS: There was not only the personal bribes, where Chirac's party, Chirac's interior minister, and a whole raft of French officials got certificates that said, You can buy Iraqi oil at 10 dollars a barrel and turn around the next day and sell it at 25 a barrel – oil that was intended to go to feed the starving children of Iraq, oil that France voted to let pump even though the United States didn't want it, and that constituted the bribe. That wasn't enough. Saddam himself went to the French and said, "I have two of the world's greatest oil fields here in Iraq that are not yet developed, and he gave one to Russia and one to China." And he said, "with these 4 oil fields, you can exploit them, they're yours the moment sanctions are lifted against me." So these members of the Security Council voted to lift sanctions. The reason we didn't have the allies we usually do is, they were on the take.

KOCH: And we should never forgive them.

MORRIS: When they needed us, we were there, in World War I, World War II, in the Cold War. And it comes with ill grace that when we needed them they just were nowhere to be seen.

ZELL MILLER

MILLER: I'm a huge baseball fan, and I knew that George Bush knew a lot about baseball.   And it's not very often that you meet someone in politics who knows anything about hitting behind the runner, but he did.   And so we hit it off from the very beginning as far as our love for baseball.   But I also was impressed with the fact that he was such a straight shooter, that he treated the First Lady with a degree of tenderness and reverence that you don't always see, and the unabashed love that he showed his daughters and his parents.   I like the fact that he's a strong man of faith who's the same kind of guy on a Saturday night that he is on a Sunday morning.   I just liked the man.

FAHRENHYPE 9/11:   Why do you consider him the right man for the job right now?

MILLER: I was one of those Americans who had grown weary of seeing our country attacked and we not responding.   I watched what happened at the World Trade Center in 1993 when the Americans were killed.   And there was no response.   I watched what happened at the Khobar Towers and what happened at the embassies in Africa.   And on each and every one of these attacks on Americans, there was absolutely no response, or an inadequate response.   It was almost as if we were sending them an engraved invitation to attack us.   And finally they did.   And I am so thankful, and America should be thankful, that George W. Bush was president at that time.   I thought that he met that challenge head on.

He's a very plain spoken man, and I think when he says that he's going to carry this fight to the enemy, the enemy knows that he's a person who will.   And I watched as he gave that speech to the joint session of congress – I think one of the most magnificent speeches that any president has ever given.   I'm a great fan of Churchill, and I had longed for a leader that had

With thanks to Cox & Forkum

a little Churchill in him. I saw that in that speech, and I saw that in his resolve after the attack on 9/11. I don't think we could have a better man. He's a man who means what he says, says what he means, has a strong backbone.

FAHRENHYPE 9/11:   Are we at war?

MILLER: Even before 9/11 we were at war, but nobody would tell us we were at war. It was kind of kept from us. Only those people who realized that Americans were being killed and that these terrorists were out there could fully appreciate it. After 9/11 people began to realize it, but up until that time we'd sort of lived in a fool's paradise, not understanding just how vulnerable we were. And we've come a long ways since 9/11. This world, this country is a lot safer than it was on 9/11.

FAHRENHYPE 9/11:   To people who say, "there's no terrorist threat, that's the biggest lie," what do you say?

MILLER: I don't know how anybody could say that and be an American, and be concerned about what happens to this country and what happens to our families. The terrorist threat is real. It's every day it's real. And I guess – I hate to say this but one of these days when another attack occurs, they're gonna realize it then, but by then it's gonna be too late.

FAHRENHYPE 9/11:   Senator you've described the Democratic party as too liberal, too elitist. How are we seeing a manifestation of that?

MILLER: You see it in just about everything, especially what happens in Congress, and what happens really throughout the country. I mean, I'd never heard the expression "What do the groups think about it?" until I went to Washington. I'd been in politics all my life, nearly 40 years. And you have these very liberal, left-leaning special interest groups who work together, they furnish the money for the Democratic party, they furnish the manpower to get out the vote, they do all these things, and then of course they expect to be repaid, in full, after the election is over.

The best example I know of, and it relates to the security of this country. We were trying to pass a Homeland Security bill. It was needed. There were 22 agencies just scattered all over the bureaucracy at the federal government. They needed to be brought together under one umbrella. That's what President Bush was trying to do. He introduced this bill – I was the only Democrat who supported it. Well the Democrats did what they do so often in the Senate – they slow walked it – that's their term, slow walking something, which means they're obstructing it, they're drawing it out. For 112 days, 11 different votes, we could not pass the Homeland Security bill in the Senate. This is in 2001 when we needed to be getting on with this job. And yet we couldn't even pass this Homeland Security bill in the Senate, because the special interests opposed it.

They wanted a provision that had to do with collective bargaining and employees' rights– that was more important to the Democrats, because it was more important to the liberal groups than the security of this country was.

It was a dumb thing to do and a terrible, dangerous thing to do for our country. That's when I quit going to Democratic caucus lunches. I said, "This is too much for me." This is the straw that breaks the camel's back.

FAHRENHYPE 9/11: In your "house divided" speech, you talked about the importance of debate, the importance of discussion, but that there comes a time, and there are things we don't divide ourselves on, that we join together, we are united and we move forward. Tell me your experience with the fight on terrorism and how we've become divided.

MILLER: The Senate is a place where an awful lot of debate and talk goes on. Always has, always will be I guess. But sometimes, when a war is going on and when lives may be lost, it's time to get things moving. The Senate did not understand that. I told a story on the Senate floor that I think explains kind of where I came from and where I think the country ought to have been coming from at that time.

I was working in my back yard cleaning out some old stacked rocks, some steps that had been there years ago. And as I was cleaning out those rocks and removing those stacked rocks, I came across a nest of copper-head snakes. Now a copperhead is a poisonous snake, it will kill you. When I came across them, I did not go before the city council and ask for a resolution. I didn't call Shirley, my wife, like I do on everything else that comes up. I didn't call any of my neighbors. I just took a hoe and chopped their heads off. Now you might call that pre-emptive action or unilateral action, but those things were dangerous. They could kill my grandchil-dren, they could kill my great-grandchildren. They play around those steps all the time. I had to do something about their safety. And that's kind of how I see this situation right now. We're in a war with a bunch of snakes, a bunch of vipers and we've got to get to them and fight it out in their neck of the woods, instead of them fighting it out in our neighborhood.

FAHRENHYPE 9/11:   When you heard Senator Powell's presentation before the U.N. stating the case against Saddam Hussein, you were moti-vated by that. That statement included information about evidence regard-ing weapons of mass destruction. Those have not been found to this day yet. Does that change how you feel about what we're doing in Iraq?

MILLER: Not one bit. Because I think what happened was, they moved those weapons of mass destruction, probably to Syria, maybe to Iran, some other places nearby, and I think they're still there in that area. I don't think there's any doubt that Saddam Hussein was doing his best to get a nuclear bomb, that he was doing his best to manufacture nuclear weapons, because he wanted to use them against us, and probably also others. And so as far as not being able to find the weapons themselves, that doesn't bother me at all because I know this man was trying to get them – he would have got-

With thanks to Linda Eddy, Iowa Presidential Watch

ten those weapons sooner or later.

FAHRENHYPE 9/11:   There is a hate out there unlike anything I've ever seen towards an elected official. Tell me about that divisiveness, that polarization, that's occurring today.

MILLER: That's a tragic situation, and I blame a lot of my Democratic colleagues for helping bring that about: the rants of Al Gore, the screams of Howard Dean, the terribly cruel and untrue things that have been said about our commander in chief in time of war. It's really unbelievable. Usually politics stops at the water's edge, and the Democrats that I knew like Harry Truman, Franklin Roosevelt, John F. Kennedy -- they were very strong on national defense. And Republicans back then helped them. Now you cannot find hardly a single Democrat who will come to the aid of a president in time of war.

I also blame the liberal news media, who without any question has a bias against this man. I don't know exactly why they don't like him. They don't like the military, I know that, and they don't like going to war. They've never seen a war that they thought solved anything, or if it did it shouldn't have. And I blame it on propagandists like Michael Moore and some of these folks we see from Hollywood like Sean Penn and Whoopi Goldberg, Susan Sarandon.

FAHRENHYPE 9/11:   You've served in the military, how does your experience compare to what we're seeing today?

MILLER: I served in the military, in the Marine Corps, back during the tail end of the Korean conflict. I was already out of the Marines and taking the benefit of the GI bill and raising a family when the Vietnam War came along, but I had a lot of friends who I'd known in the Marine Corps who fought in it. And what happened with those veterans when they came back home to an ungrateful nation, is one of the great disgraces. And I think that there are too many American politicians today, particularly in my party, who are sort of these long in the tooth '60s liberals who see everything defined by the Vietnam War.

Well, the Vietnam War is just one of the lessons of history. There are a lot of lessons of history. There are the ovens of Auschwitz, there's Pearl Harbor, there's those skies over Berlin, there's Iwo Jima and those mountain ridges in Korea, and those mass graves in the Iraqi desert, and there's also those halls of the Pentagon and that grassy ridge in Pennsylvania, and those towers in Manhattan that went up in smoke. Those are the real lessons of history, not just the Vietnam War.

FAHRENHYPE 9/11:   What is your hope for the Democratic Party?

MILLER: There ought to be room in the Democratic Party for liberals and conservatives, and there ought to be room in the Republican Party for liberals and conservatives. Once, that was the case. Jacob Javits was a great Republican Senator from New York and he was very, very liberal. Richard Russell was a great Senator from Georgia and he was very, very conservative. Sam Irvin who lives not too far from these mountains, he was a conservative Democratic and I think everyone would say he was a great American and a great Democratic. Howard Baker, who also lives not far from where we're standing right now, he was a more moderate Republican.

I'm a Democrat because I was born a Democrat. In this area of Georgia and North Carolina and Tennessee, there's always been a strong two party system. It goes all the way back to the Civil War. And it used to be, you tell me a person's name from around here and I could tell you about his last name, whether he was a Democrat or a Republican -- they were just born that way. That's not the case now. If you're conservative like I am, the Democrats want to throw you out. They don't think there's any room for you under than big umbrella. What was once a big umbrella is narrowed down now to the size of a dunce cap.

Right now I've got a lot of Democrats who have a bull's eye painted on my back as if I were some kind of traitor to the party. I hope they would understand that I have voted for every Democratic presidential candidate since 1952, 13 of them. I have voted for over 600 Democratic state and local officials. I have never voted for a Republican until here in 2004, when I'm gonna vote for George W. Bush's re-election. And the reason I'm gonna do that is not because he's a Republican. The reason I'm gonna do that is because he's the person who can best protect my family. I'm putting family before party. That's what I'm doing.

FAHRENHYPE 9/11:   What is your list of reasons why you're voting for George Bush?

MILLER: He will best protect my family in a time of war, and make no mistake about it: we are at war. We could be attacked by the terrorists at any day now, at any time. They are out there waiting for a good opportunity. This country is much safer because George W. Bush has been president. Before 2001 and what happened on 9/11, we had 33 air marshals on all of the flights in the whole United States. Today we've got thousands of air marshals, so many that the number's classified, and they're armed, and they're on every flight. We've got cockpit doors that have been reinforced, and floors of cockpits that have been reinforced. We've got video cameras where they can see back in the cabin.

Before 9/11, there was hardly any vaccine; today we've got billions of doses stockpiled. We've got enough smallpox vaccine for every man, woman and child in the United States, and we hardly had any before 9/11. We've taken out or made neutral countries like Iraq where the Taliban ruled and where Al Qaida trained. That's changed. Pakistan, where they did most of their recruiting, now is more friendly to the United States. That's changed. The Saudis had helped the terrorists by raising money for them. That's changed. Qaddafi has suddenly gotten religion and he's no longer harboring terrorists or seeking to acquire a nuclear bomb. It's a much safer country, and it's safer because George W. Bush had the discipline and made

With thanks to Linda Eddy, Iowa Presidential Watch

hard choices.

FAHRENHYPE 9/11:   Do you agree with everything George Bush does?

MILLER: I don't agree with everything George Bush does. I don't agree with everything that the Republicans do in Congress. I vote with the Republicans a lot, not because they're Republicans but because they're conservatives.

FAHRENHYPE 9/11: Are the Democrats trying to hide something? Are they ashamed of something?

MILLER: I think liberalism to a certain extent, both in foreign affairs and domestic affairs, has been somewhat discredited by what's happened over the last 30 years. I can remember when they thought Jimmy Carter's pacifism was the answer. Well, they were wrong. I can remember when they thought that Ronald Reagan's conservatism was wrong. Well, they were wrong. I can remember when they thought that reforming welfare would not have any positive results. It's had tremendous positive results. I think a lot of their ideas have been discredited over the years, but unfortunately these liberal special interest groups grow richer by the day and have more money to pour into campaigns than they've ever had before, and so they therefore keep them alive.

ANN COULTER

DICK MORRIS: Michael Morris told a University of Michigan student newspaper, "There is no terrorist threat in this country. This is a lie. This is the biggest lie we've been told."

ANN COULTER: What can you say to something like that?

MORRIS: Maybe we should interview him in the crater of the World Trade Center. Maybe we should take Mr. Moore on a guided tour of all of the buildings that wouldn't be standing if we hadn't broken up this terrorist threat that doesn't exist. We'd begin by walking him over the Brooklyn Bridge, as opposed to having to swim. Then we'd take him to Wall Street where he undoubtedly trades stocks. Then we'd take him to the garment center where they wanted to blow up all of midtown Manhattan. Then we'd take him the Citicorp Center, the IMF building, the World Bank building. We'd take him to all these places where the terrorist threat doesn't exist.

COULTER: It didn't start with 9/11. That was the most spectacular attack within America's borders on American soil, but this has been going on for 20 years. I mean, I don't know what you say to that. It's like someone saying, "the sun rises in the west and sets in the east." It's been attack, attack, attack. The Khobar Towers, the embassy bombings, the attacks on our troops in Saudi Arabia, the West Berlin discotheque, the two attacks on the World Trade Center. Although we don't know much publicly about what's been happening, the Bush administration has been rounding up terrorist groups in this country.

MORRIS: Moore does an interview with the London Mirror on November 3rd, 2003, and again I'm quoting,: "I want Bush paraded in handcuffs outside the police house as a common criminal. I've never seen anything like Bush and his people. They truly hate our constitution, our rights and our liberties. They have no shame in fighting for their corporate sponsors."

COULTER: Well at least there is some public official that he considers guilty, since he's not sure that Osama bin Laden is guilty. He famously said in Aspen to a standing ovation that Bin Laden may be innocent. So it's good you know he thinks some public official is definitely guilty, and that's George Bush. He says Bush lied, lied! I enthusiastically support liberals for finally deciding lying is a bad thing. That's a step in the right direction. But we need to explain to them what a lie is. When a president makes a prediction about the future that turns out to be untrue, that's not a lie, that's making an incorrect prediction. You know, my prediction that the Yankees would win the 2003 World Series, that's a lie, it's a lie, in fact it's a contemptible lie.

MORRIS: After the Gulf War, Saddam Hussein admitted that he had all of these weapons of mass destruction. The U.N. inspectors came in and made him dismantle. Then only 3 or 4 years ago he got the right to pump oil and the right to keep the money and use it for rearmament. And you've got Michael Moore saying it's a lie that Saddam wants to develop weapons of mass destruction, it's a lie that he's a threat, it's a lie that he wants to attack people, his neighbors and the United States. Some lie.

COULTER: You do start to wonder about the motives of these people. I mean, you can certainly be patriotic and oppose the war with Iraq, but not based on a series of lies. When someone is engaging in public discourse and lies about it, that does not help democracy, that does not help the exchange of ideas.

I mean it's curious that the standard of evidence liberals demand before America can take action in America's defense, is an incredibly high standard, one that could not be met in any court of law.

With thanks to Cox & Forkum

MORRIS: I think you're right about the idea that someone can oppose the war without being unpatriotic.   But you think you can say this without being unpatriotic, in an interview with a Japanese newspaper: "The Iraqis who have risen up against the occupation – that's us, the occupation – are not insurgents or terrorists or the enemy. They are the revolution, the minutemen, and their numbers will grow, and they will win." Can you say that without being unpatriotic? Michael Moore did.

COULTER: No I think you could win that in a court of law. It's amazing, these savages slaughtering innocents, slaughtering civilians, trying to prevent democracy from coming to fruition in Iraq. I mean whether or not you think it was worth America going in, and shedding blood to create a democracy there, no one can contest that it would be a better thing. What could be worse than living under Saddam Hussein?

MORRIS: I think that the whole argument that lies behind Moore's thesis, which is that we're sacrificing blood for oil flies in the face of 3 fundamental facts. Number 1—

COULTER: Gas has gone up. Why are gas prices so high if we went to war for oil?

MORRIS: Number 1, we support Israel that doesn't have any oil, and we oppose the Arabs, who have it all. Number 2, we don't buy Iranian oil. We're the only country in the world that boycotts Iranian oil. And number 3, for 15 years we opposed letting Iraq pump oil.

COULTER: And why are gas prices so high? If I were a liberal, my conspiracy theory is that the reason gas is so expensive is that George Soros is fiddling with the market to get George Bush out of power. Let's throw that one around the Internet.

MORRIS: I just think that the whole concept that they hate us because we're a bully, because we're a global bad boy, because we throw our weight around globally -- I think that's so crazy. I think they hate us because we have free speech, we have free religion, we support the most persecuted people on the face of the earth throughout history, Israel. And we don't treat women as sex objects and we give them rights. That's why they hate us.

COULTER: My friend Eleanor Burquette, a liberal in good standing, wrote the book So Many Enemies, So Little Time, after having traveled in many of the Axis of Evil countries. And she says they hate us because we're the prom queen. You want to become Uganda, they'll love us. But as long as we are the most powerful free wealthy country in the world, some people are going to hate us.

MORRIS: So why does Michael Moore hate us?

COULTER: You may need to bring in a shrink for that one. Or an exorcist.

MORRIS: I think he fills the market.

COULTER: Yes, there is something about these leftists who so intensely hate America. They seem to think that nuclear annihilation will not affect them. I mean it is part of their elitism, their feeling that they're above the world, they're not normal Americans. What protects me in this world as a humble middle class person is the fact that I am an American. That gives me certain rights and privileges. I love this country not only for its freedom and, and its foundation that all men are created equal, but it literally protects me, being an American citizen. Oh, but not if you're Barbra Streisand, not if you're Michael Moore. Oh no, you are so fabulously rich it doesn't matter if the world explodes, you will still have your hacienda on the beach and your beachfront property. This is what they brag about. It's boastful, these anti-American ideas, and one world government. They don't care about America, they don't need America, they're too cool to need America.

MORRIS: Michael Moore said to the British in Liverpool: "It's all part of the same ball of wax, right? The oil companies, Israel, Halliburton."

COULTER: It's curious how nuts people are with conspiracy theories. I mean we can go out on the street right now and find a guy with a tin foil cap on. And he not only think the CIA is beaming into his fillings, but it somehow involves the Jews.

MORRIS: That's right. And he said that the way we can stop suicide bombings is to give the Palestinians a bunch of missile-firing Apache helicopters, and let them and the Israelis go at each other, head to head, four billion dollars a year to Israel, four billion a year to the Palestinians, they can just blow each other up and leave the rest of us the hell alone—

COULTER: Give guns to Palestinians so they can slaughter Israelis? This is the guy who's worried that you can buy a gun in America and go to a shooting range? Isn't he Mr. Anti-Gun? And he's calling for a holocaust among Palestinians and Israelis?

MORRIS: Does anybody here seriously believe that if the Arabs were not attacking Israel, Israel would attack the Arabs? Is there anybody who seriously believes the Israelis enjoy sending tanks into the West Bank? Or that they're building a wall for exercise? Does anybody really believe that this is not a one way war?

COULTER: America does take the side of the innocent beleaguered against

With thanks to Linda Eddy, Iowa Presidential Watch

the savages… You have a population of a few million Jews precariously holding on to the edge of the Mediterranean, and Arabs can't sleep at night!

MORRIS: Right! It goes back to the culture of blame that I think animates Arab countries. Not Muslim countries, that's wrong. Turkey it doesn't, Indonesia it doesn't, Philippines it doesn't.

COULTER: And Morocco it doesn't.

MORRIS: Bernard Lewis wrote that the suicide bomber could become the metaphor for the entire Arab world. It's this culture of blame. And you know, anti-Semitism in the United States always advances masked. Nobody gets up there and says, I hate the Jews. What they say is, "The Jews control the media, the Jews control the banks, the Jews control the establishment."

And then we get to the Patriot Act. He likens it to Mein Kampf. He says, "The Patriot Act is the first step. Mein Kampf was written long before Hitler came to power. If people don't speak up against this, you end up with something like they had in Germany."

COULTER: I love this, from the man who supports Hezbollah, who supports Palestinian suicide bombers, who dedicated his book to that American protestor burning American flags with the Palestinians, whose jacket flap endorsement on Stupid White Men came from that ferocious anti-Semite who actually was asked not to give a speech at Harvard…who said horrible things, horrible things about how'd he'd like to kill a Jew in Brooklyn. Well he's one of the jacket flap endorsements on Michael Moore's book. So what, now he's complaining about Mein Kampf? Well now that's odd – he doesn't like it 50 years ago, but he wants it now?

MORRIS: I think the suicide bombings are the holocaust on the installment plan. I mean they have lost 750 people in a country with a population of 5 million. So you do the math – that's as if the United States was going to lose 40,000 to 50,000 people, the equivalent of our losses in Vietnam.

COULTER: It's hideous. I feel sorry for the peaceful Palestinians who would like to just have a homeland. I think they should have a homeland, and Israel would give it to them, and would give it to them tomorrow, but you can't win by engaging in suicide bombings. The civilized world cannot accept that.

MORRIS: Now Dustin Hoffman says, "The war is about hegemony, money and power and oil." What do you think of that?

COULTER: I demand that he spell and define hegemony.

MORRIS: And when Sean Penn says, "If there's a war or continued sanctions against Iraq, the blood of Americans and Iraqis alike will be on American hands." And this is when we're trying to topple Saddam Hussein. I mean, I just don't think you could make the case that Saddam Hussein is a nicer man than Adolf Hitler. I think that you could basically say they're parallel. The death toll is parallel given the size of the countries. Germany occupied a continent of 200 or 300 million people and killed 12 million Jews and others in camps. Iraq has a country of 19 million people, and he's killed roughly a million to a million and a half Iranians, Kuwaitis and Iraqis.

COULTER: Oh that's interesting.

MORRIS: So it's about the same order of magnitude. Now if we take that sentence and we just change the words: If there is a war or continued sanctions against Nazi Germany, the blood of Americans and Germans alike will be on American hands. I mean, how does that sound?

COULTER: And I'll pay a thousand dollars for any liberal who will ever mention the Kurds. That never passes their lips. See the Kurds actually are dancing and cheering in the streets. We don't have any troops in the Kurdish controlled area, because I mean you did have Saddam engaging in, in genocide against the Kurds. Liberals claim that they're happy Saddam is gone, the same way they claim to support the troops. It's just one of these statements they make. They feel the American people would demand that they say it, but they clearly do not believe.

When liberals look at war, they want to run and hide. It does make you wonder, can America ever fight a war if liberals have their way? I mean, the Battle of Iwo Jima took 17,000 men over a few weeks. 17,000 men – that's a single battle. And the country went on and won the war. And now it's carp, carp, carp, carp, carp, carp. We lost a thousand and God bless those brave men, and we can sit warm and happy.

MORRIS: Importantly, the whole thrust of what we're doing in Iraq has been to minimize deaths. The Pentagon doesn't need precision guided munitions. They could just drop a big bomb and blow everything up. The reason we have precision guided munitions is to minimize civilian casualties.

COULTER: We know we can flatten any city in 10 minutes. The Pentagon can call that in. What's amazing about this war is how this military can go in strategically, protect mosques, protect civilians – at risk to itself, and the bravery of our troops – it's an amazing war. And if, if this is what liberals are going to quit over, then there's no war we can ever fight.

MORRIS: Why the anger, Anne? Is it just that conservatives hated Clinton and liberals hate Bush, and we're in a permanent era of partisan hatred, and we're incapable of opposition without that level of animus? Or is there some psychology going on in the left that makes them hate George Bush?

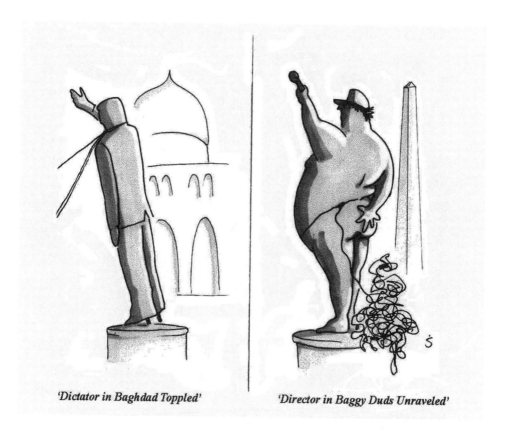

'Dictator in Baghdad Toppled'   'Director in Baggy Duds Unraveled'

With thanks to Juju Dandridge Suits

I voted for Al Gore. I would now vote for George Bush for re-election. I like what Bush has done in terror. I don't like most of his domestic policies.

COULTER: I'm not wild about a lot of 'em.

MORRIS: But the hate is inappropriate, I think. What causes it?

COULTER: Part of it is retaliation for Clinton, though as a member in good standing of the Clinton haters, there wasn't this animosity. If anything, we thought he was kind of funny. We laughed at him, we made fun of him, we thought it was appalling that this man was sitting in the Oval Office. But hatred, no. Part of it is this retaliation. Part of it is the 2000 election. They have persuaded themselves that Gore won.

MORRIS: The reason Al Gore lost the election was not the electoral college, it was not ballot fraud, it was the 2.7 percent of the liberals who voted for Ralph Nader.

COULTER: Let's hope they do it again! The real reason I think the left hates George Bush with an intensity I have never seen before is because he's a Christian. They hated Ronald Reagan for the same reason, but they convinced themselves that "Reagan doesn't really believe it – he doesn't go to church, he has this phony excuse about needing Secret Service protection."

Truth is, anyone who looks at Reagan's oeuvre knows that he really believed in God. In fact the end of the 1980 Republican National Convention, at the end of his convention speech he said words to the effect of, "I was afraid to say this tonight, but I'm more afraid if I don't. We're at a crossroads in our national history, and I ask you all to engage in a minute of prayer. Prayer. Not a moment of silence, prayer." And the entire convention hall did it. It's stunning!

You can't even imagine Bush doing it today, they've so cowed him on

Christianity. But they know that Bush is a real Christian, they have a live one this time. And I think they really hate that.

MORRIS: I think that what's going on from the left's point of view is that there is a sense of what should happen: we should be opposing terror, we should be honoring the 9/11 victims, we should believe in God, we should be spiritual people – there are all these should's. And they feel left out, they feel that their political opposition is being marginalized, not just as wrong but as sacrilegious, unpatriotic, defiling of the victims. And they feel that the whole country is going one way and they're left outside, and they're becoming more and more bitter in that exclusion.

COULTER: I think there is a lot to that. They think they speak for their own little silent majority: Oh no, no, no, oh no. I mean when they run a convention where they have to lie about what their beliefs are, as they did at the Democratic National Convention. Kerry would say, "we need more Head Start, Early Start, Jump Start – and huge standing ovations – yea, yea! We'll fight the terrorists— boo, I mean yea! It was so phony. I mean when you have to run a convention when you're lying to the American people on your beliefs, you know what direction the country is going in. They could well go the way of the Wigs. This is a party that is marginalized, and it could be the death rattle.

MORRIS: After 9/11, Susan Sarandon charged that Bush has hijacked our pain, our loss, our fear. And it seems to me that that is really what the left is saying: we felt pain, we felt loss, we feel fear. And you – and these are universal emotions that everybody except Michael Moore maybe feels, in the United States – and you're telling us that those emotions have to lead to certain policy and political conclusions. And we resent that you're using our own feelings to lead us to someplace where intellectually we don't want to go, and therefore we react viscerally against it.

COULTER: That's a good explanation, but I think a little too intellectual for the characters we're talking about here. I think they felt pain, but they felt pain because they were no longer the focus of page 6, they were no longer the focus of the mass's attention: "Oh what is Susan Sarandon doing today?" "And what was she wearing to this event or that event?" "And what happened at the Calvin Klein fashion show?" Suddenly they were off the news pages, and I think that was painful for them.

MORRIS: Yes, and there has been a virtual monopoly on culture, on pop art and society in New York and Los Angeles. Despite the fact that New York was eviscerated by terror, New Yorkers and L.A. types tend – or at least Hollywood types, tend not to share the Bush Administration's agenda. So in a sense, this is America rearing its ugly head. I remember during the Clinton campaign, I told him "let's advertise really early to get you re-elected." And he said, "People will criticize me, they'll say I'm too weak, they'll say I'm doing this because I'm desperate." And I said back to him, "you are too weak and you are desperate." And he said, "I'm going to take a hit for that." And I said "don't worry, we've got it covered – we won't advertise in New York and Washington"—

COULTER: And no one will know!

MORRIS: You can advertise in half the country three times a week, and nobody will know. For 18 months we never advertised in New York or D.C., and nothing appeared in the press. It was only revealed after the election when I wrote it in my book. We spent 40 million dollars, and nobody noticed! So in a sense, is this "the rest of America" thinking for itself in a way that the elites on each coast tend to object to?

COULTER: Their entire Democratic party stands for violating each one of the 10 commandments one by one by one, ripping them out of courthouses, down from public parks and schools.

With thanks to Larry Wright, The Detroit News

MORRIS: I don't agree with that but—

COULTER: I'll bring you over.

MORRIS: But I do think there is a, a fundamental lack of belief in evil –

COULTER: Agreed, I think they embrace it.

MORRIS: It's one thing to say, "Saddam Hussein was bad but blah, blah, blah." First of all, they say sanctions would have gotten rid of Saddam Hussein. Give me a break. First of all, there were no sanctions, they were lifted entirely. Saddam Hussein was able to get as much money from the Oil for Food Program as he bloody well wanted. So it was not a question of give sanctions a chance. By the time Clinton left office, there effectively were no sanctions on Iraq.

COULTER: That's interesting. I didn't realize that.

MORRIS: Well what does Iraq make? Oil. And the maximum they could ever pump is 3 million barrels of oil. They were pumping and selling 3 million barrels of oil. So what sanctions?

COULTER: I see, so we had sanctions on like little trinkets they'd make.

MORRIS: Yeah, they can't export their beads. So the point, there were no sanctions and that left essentially no plans for getting rid of Saddam Hussein. So did he cause 9/11? Well I go back to the other question – did Germany cause Pearl Harbor? Was that the Luftwaffe? No, it was the Japanese Air Force. And I don't care what type of terrorism Saddam Hussein practiced, I don't care if there was a secular one or if it was a religious one and Iran is a Shiite one, and Saudi Arabia is a Wahhabi one – I don't care what brand it is. It's terrorism. And those terrorist forces interact, coalesce—

COULTER: I love these fine distinctions liberals will make among the different breeds of Islamic fundamentalism and America hating. Why can they never see those distinctions when they're talking about like George Bush and Rush Limbaugh? No that's a blur to them. But Shiites versus Baathists versus the Secularists – I mean these fine distinctions they can make in that case.

MORRIS: A terrorist gang is like an HIV virus. It swims through your bloodstream, and it can't do you any real harm. I mean a terrorist gang can blow up a mailbox or they can plant a bomb or they can pull off a suicide bombing, but it's only when the HIV virus latches onto a cell and uses the DNA of the cell that you get sick and it spreads throughout your body. And similarly, a terrorist gang latches onto a country like Afghanistan or like Iraq, Iran. And then it uses the accoutrements of nationhood – secure borders, a conscript population they can press into service, a navy and an air force, intelligence missions around the world, diplomatic missions, export/import trade, foreign currency reserves, secure borders – that's what makes it possible for a gang who could blow up a mailbox to blow up the World Trade Center.

Because the HIV virus changes form so often, it becomes a very different virus each time. And the terrorist gang changes its leadership, changes its membership, and it's futile to swim after it and try to catch it. The key thing is to stop it from taking over a cell. That's how we prevent AIDS and it's how we can prevent terrorism. So the genius of George Bush was to say, "Who are the nation receptors that would take a terrorist gang in? Well there's Afghanistan because they have the Taliban. There's Saddam Hussein because he hates us anyway, he has all of this oil and we know he's willing to do anything to get us. There's Syria because of their leadership. There's Iran because they say so. There's North Korea because they say so." And maybe a blind spot about Saudi Arabia. Then we go to each of those cells and reinforce that membrane and change them so they can't receive the HIV virus.

COULTER: That is brilliant. That is the problem with something like Afghanistan or Iraq. Even if liberals will deny the numerous connections between Al Qaida and Iraq, the point is that without a serious adult, quasi-democratic government in these countries you have lunatics like Osama bin Laden running wild. Actually, a war in Afghanistan is less justifiable in some ways than Iraq. It's not like that was always Osama's home. He had just moved there from the Sudan. He's a lunatic moving from country to country. We need to create an Arab Israel, and that's what we're doing in Iraq.

MORRIS: An Arab Israel. What a fascinating idea. You mean a democracy that spreads democracy.

COULTER: Right, right. A government we can deal with.

MORRIS: And it's worth realizing that whenever radical Islamic principles have been put up for a vote, they've always lost. They got 9 percent in Pakistan, 2 to 5 percent in Iran—

COULTER: Right, most people want to live in freedom.

MORRIS: Let's go back to the phenomenon in the United States. You know, it's a metaphor, but it's really true, that you fly from New York to L.A. and you do the trip in 5 or 6 hours, and you get in one airport and you get in the other airport, and it's easy to treat the country like an accordion, collapse it so that there's New York and there's L.A., and there's nothing in between. Isn't that the basis of the Moore movie, to forget what's in between, to take an accordion and collapse the country?

"He is icky; but his millions are attractive."

With thanks to Juju Dandridge Suits

COULTER: It's certainly what the movie does. I notice from talking to my friends in L.A. and New York that they're a whole lot more pessimistic about this next election than I am. I go to America and I see Americans, and it's a different country out there. It's also a much better country out there.

MORRIS: Do you think that one of the fundamental distinctions between Michael Moore and the American people is that we believe America is good, and he believes America is bad?

COULTER: Oh absolutely. He thinks we're Mein Kampf, going around creating evil, killing innocents.

MORRIS: He says to the British, You're stuck with being connected to this country of mine, which is known for bringing sadness and misery to places around the globe.

COULTER: I would like to have a court case on who loves his country more, me or Michael Moore. You could win that in court. This is a man who goes around telling slanderous lies about his own country. He can say as much as he wants – he supports the troops, he loves his country, he wishes Saddam were gone – well it's not true. You can't say you love your country and then go around slandering it, telling vicious horrible lies about it.

In a worst case scenario, if everything that Michael Moore and Al Franken and George Soros believe is true, and there is not one single virus sitting in any Iraqi mad scientist's lab, then this was a purely humanitarian war. We have freed people from a mad dictator. I thought they claimed to support that.

MORRIS: And let's go through the catalog of misery that we spread throughout the world. Such as our soldiers storming Omaha Beach bringing misery and destruction. Or when the United States subsidized AIDS research, developed solutions to the disease, and now works to make them available throughout the world at as low a price as we possibly can. Is that spreading misery and destruction? When the United States takes the lead in granting free trade throughout the world, is that misery and destruction?

COULTER: And freed millions of people in the Soviet Union.

MORRIS: When we risked American lives to stop genocide in Bosnia, was that misery and destruction? When we saved Kuwait, when we freed Iraq from the vicious grip of Saddam Hussein's dictatorship, was that misery and destruction?

COULTER: They say "Oh no, we love our country, don't you dare say I'm not patriotic." And then they go around and attack it. They say "don't confuse dissent with treason." Well okay, then don't confuse treason with dissent.

MORRIS: When George Clooney says, "The government itself is running exactly like The Sopranos"—

COULTER: An analogy like that can only come out of Hollywood.

MORRIS: The entire concept that America is evil, I think that really lies at the core of what Michael Moore is saying. It is not a good country that's making a mistake, which a lot of good people believe about the war in Iraq. It's not a good country that was misled on its priorities, which a lot of good people believe about Iraq. His view is, "we are a bad country, an evil country, doing its thing."

The other thing I find incredible about Michael Moore's approach is the ridiculing, the humiliating, the putdowns of American soldiers. The way he goes through that movie and makes them the bad guys in an effort to stir up the demonization of American troops that took place during Vietnam.

COULTER: I think the problem with this sort of thing is the lies. You really have to question a man's motives when he lies in formulating an argument. You can't trust him with anything. Simple things like reversing the order in which quotes were given, like cutting a tape, open lies about how many in Congress have children in the military. In fact, the children of politicians are more likely to have children in the military. But Moore just lies about it.

To laugh at the passengers on the flights of 9/11, as Michael Moore did in his stand up act in England, calling them scaredy cats, and this suck up to the "brothers" whom he thinks he's so close to, the blacks he's constantly fawning over, and saying that if there had been blacks on the planes they wouldn't have let him get away with this, it's just contemptible!

MORRIS: We have a lot of tasks before us. We have to deal with Iran, we have to deal with the craziest regime on the planet getting a nuclear weapon. We have to deal with the most isolated, hermetically sealed regime there is, North Korea, getting nuclear weapons.

COULTER: I was going to say that the second craziest already has one.

MORRIS: Right. And no foreign enemy has ever defeated the United States on the battlefield. They defeat us in public opinion. And I did not question Moore's motivation. I give him the same credit for his motivation and his patriotism that I give to John Kerry and John Edwards and Bill Clinton and Al Gore, even if I gave him that, 9/11 is a dangerous film because it undermines our morale, it saps our reserve, and it erodes that sense of our own virtue, of the difference between good and evil that has to animate us in these times. It leads to a kind of existential feeling that every-

body's bad, everybody's terrible—

COULTER: Except Palestinian suicide bombers.

MORRIS: And that erodes our sense of the difference between good and evil when it is necessary to have a sense of good to defeat evil.

COULTER: That's absolutely right. You can't have a public debate based on lies. That really is an essential part of democracy. You can have your position, but when it's built on this web of lies, it does call into question your motivation. But it also clutters public discourse. America does have a messianic place in the world. We do spread freedom and the idea that all men are created equal. Sometimes, when necessary, with guns and troops, and sometimes with foreign aid. But America is different from any other country. It is the only non-imperialist superpower in the history of the world, and if that's gone, I mean forget about you and me, forget about this country, it doesn't bode well for the world.

MORRIS: It really is a question of a very, very different approach by a world power. The Wall Street Journal had an article a month or two ago that was fascinating. It said when Britain was running the world, its strategy was to sell as much to other people and make as much money as you can, and own as much from other countries so that you own them.

But what the United States does is the precise opposite. We buy as much from other countries as we possibly can, so we're not their biggest seller, we're their best customer. And we let them invest as much money as they want buying American companies and American land. And it gives us a wonderful role in the world, because countries will alienate their seller, but they won't alienate their best customer. And they will resent it when you own them, but they'll protect it when they own you. And in a sense it's this entire American construct, which is that we do better in a world that's free than a world which we control.

COULTER: It's very inspiring when you hear George Bush say how he believes most people yearn to be free. You see it in places like Iraq. Whatever horrible propaganda they've been subjected to, people do yearn to be free.

MORRIS: But in Michael Moore's movie, he has the 7 minutes where the President just sat there after he was told the second plane had hit. What do you say to that?

COULTER: I would like liberals to explain to me what they think George Bush should have done – you know, run out of the classroom, rip open his shirt: Let the bullets hit me first! They're so childlike. For one thing, we didn't know what was going on. It was very public where the president was. The school has to be secured. You have to get Air Force One ready. Where are the terrorists? They're in air space, they're in the skies, all of this has to be secured, the school has got to be secured. What's he going to do? Make a pay phone call? Call from his cell phone to Dick Cheney? He is the President of the United States, we don't need a presidential assassination in that 7 minutes. I'm quite sure the Secret Service wouldn't have let him run out and run around the school or do whatever liberals think he should be doing. But that is the sort of thing they latch themselves onto.

Furthermore, what was the big rush? Michael Moore now claims he supported war with Afghanistan, but as I say, in December 2001 he was getting standing ovations from the Aspen crowds saying he wasn't sure if Osama bin Laden was guilty. Well then, what was Bush going to rush to do? Rush to attack Afghanistan, where there was a possibly innocent man, Osama bin Laden? Attack Iraq, which Michael Moore also opposed? What did they want him to do?

MORRIS: If I could talk to people who had just seen *Fahrenheit 9/11*, the first thing I would do is tell them, "please don't lose faith in the United States of America. We're a much better country than he portrays. We're much better motivated. We don't do this stuff for oil, we don't do this stuff for money, we don't like to inflict pain on other people. We are not an imperialist country, we're not the Roman Empire. Don't lose faith in yourself. Because if you lose faith in yourself, in your own country, the United States, you've undermined the only really consistent force for good in the world."

COULTER: I would cite one of the most egregious lies -- for example, to show American troops laughing at a man with a shroud over his head, lying in the street in Iraq as if they're laughing at someone who's being tortured, when it was just a drunk who had fallen down on the streets, and to create hatred toward American troops, that is a lie. It is designed to make you hate your country, and it is lie.

With thanks to Mike Lester, The Rome News-Tribune

PETER KING

DICK MORRIS: Peter, you are a Republican member of Congress from New York State, from Long Island. Many, many members of your district and friends of yours were killed in 9/11. You're not a right-wing partisan, but a quintessential moderate and centrist. That's important when you're rebutting an extremist on the left who claims that he's only opposed by extremists on the right.

PETER KING: I agree. I've always considered myself the independent, setting myself apart of any wing or any faction. But to me Michael Moore symbolizes the worst in American politics.   There's an inherent anti-Americanism in his belief. I know that's one of those pat phrases you're not supposed to use, but it really is inherent that we can have honest disagreements about the war on terrorism, about whether we should be in Afghanistan, Iraq, whether or not there should be an Axis of Evil – all of those are legitimate questions. Michael Moore goes right to the integrity of the United States. He basically accuses us of being a colonial power, he encourages the enemy, he refers to Iraqi terrorists as being freedom fighters, or compares them to the American soldiers in the Revolution. To me, it shows his true colors.

MORRIS: To call the United States a colonial power is just absurd. The United States has always opposed colonialism, never had colonies. The last thing in the world we want is to have to have responsibility for Iraq or Afghanistan. We'd love to be out of there as fast as we can.

KING: In fact if there's any criticism that's valid of the United States over the years, it's that we tend to be an isolationist power. And after World War II I think the mistake we made is we immediately demobilized, and that allowed the Russians, the Soviets, to fortify themselves in eastern Europe.

But it was our instinct to demobilize, to bring the troops home.

MORRIS: That's a key point. The thing that stops the United States from being a hegemonic power, a colonialist power, is our sense of isolationism. You talk to a European and that's something they don't understand. Because in a tiny little country in Europe, to be an isolationist is crazy. I mean what, is Luxembourg gonna be an isolationist when they're a city, or Belgium, you take a day's walk and you're in another country – it's absurd. But in the United States there is this feeling of wanting to be left alone, wanting just to be able to do our thing in the way that we want without having a problem.

KING: I think too many countries, especially in Europe, judge us by their history. Almost every country in Europe, any large country -- Germany, France, Britain -- they've all been colonial powers. Our history is to be inward, and not to be expanding out.

A real criticism of the United States, again showing our isolationism, was that we pulled out of Afghanistan so quickly in 1989, where we were the ones who basically brought about the defeat of the Soviets. We supplied the mujadin, we supported the Afghan guerillas. If ever we wanted to serve ourselves, we could have moved in then. But we don't want to be an occupying power.

MORRIS: I think that the current take on colonialism in America is that it's commercial colonialism, that we don't want to own these countries, but we want to get their oil. And I don't think people realize that the number one foreign importer of oil to the United States is Canada. Number two is Mexico. Number three is Venezuela. We get almost no oil from the Middle East. We were the ones that opposed letting Iraq pump oil. We were the ones that opposed buying Iranian oil – we refuse to this day to buy Iranian oil. We don't need Middle Eastern oil. We produce domestically half of our oil needs.

KING: Again this whole thing that Iraq was a war for oil, that's just propaganda that's put out by honest dupes and others such as Michael Moore
who just want to put a moral cloud over everything we do.

If ever the Bush family had a chance to assert an oil monopoly, it would
have been when the Russians pulled out of Afghanistan in 1989 and 1990,
and we had no interest in doing it.

MORRIS: And there's no oil in Bosnia, there's no oil in Haiti, there's no oil
in Kosovo, there's no oil in any of the places that we've intervened, except
in the Middle East, and we don't get any of that oil.

KING: No, and in fact in Iraq, the first thing we tried to do is get the oil
pipelines up and running so the Iraqis can own their own oil. So—

MORRIS: Now I'm looking at your lapel. I've seen you with that pin
before. Please explain to us what it is.

KING: There was a large number of people in my district who were killed
on 9/11 – well over 100 and it almost 200 when you add friends and relatives from adjoining areas. There were two brothers in my district, Tim
Haskell and Tom Haskell, who were killed. I gave the eulogies at their
funerals. And their other brother was also a firefighter, who survived. He
gave me the pin, asked me to wear it, and I've worn it ever since.

MORRIS: Do you think the surviving Haskell brother would agree with
Michael Moore that there's no terrorist threat in the United States, that that's
the biggest lie we're being told?

KING: I can tell you very, very definitely that Ken Haskell, if he had
Michael Moore in the room right now, he'd strangle him.

With thanks to John Pritchett

MORRIS: Why would he strangle him?

KING: They identified totally with President Bush. They admire his leadership. Even more than that, they believe that the United States was attacked on September 11th by enemies, and that the president and the armed forces are trying to avenge those deaths and then trying to make the world safe from terrorism, and they just terribly hate and resent these attacks upon the United States made by people such as Michael Moore.

So often we hear that 9/11 families are against President Bush, and I can tell you, the overwhelming majority of 9/11 families that I've dealt with – and politics have never been an issue, but just in bringing it up, the overwhelming majority strongly support the president. They're either going to vote for him or they have great admiration for him. There's virtually none who have any animosity toward him.

MORRIS: As a congressman who represents a district on Long Island, which is one of the suburbs of New York City, where a great many of the firefighters, police officers and other people that worked at the World Trade Center lived, you've had a chance to monitor their emotions over the last 3 years, to understand how they felt on 9/11, how they felt in the aftermath, and how they've felt over the last two or three years of the various government efforts to protect them—

KING: The one thing I've never detected was an anti-American feeling. I've never heard anybody blame the United States, or blame President Bush. They didn't feel like there was any American conspiracy. The enemy was bin Laden, the enemy was Islamic terrorism, Islamic fundamentalism, that was the enemy. And what struck me the most was, after September 11th, how resolute President Bush was. I remember being at a wake for one of the firefighters, and the family started to come after me, and I thought they were going to criticize the United States. But no, they were afraid that Congress would not stand with the President, and they thought the media were going to be dragging us back.

For instance during the Afghan War, if Bill Clinton or Al Gore had been President, we would have been calling it off for Ramadan, any time there was a civilian death we'd be pulling back and apologizing. There's none of that with President Bush, and the families respect that.

They also respect the Patriot Act. There's all this talk about librarians being locked up – that is so much on the fringes. If I went to families that I know from 9/11 and said, "Are you offended by the Patriot Act?" they'd probably vote me out of office. They want more of that type of toughness. Not in a macho way, not even in a revenge way. But they realize we are on the crosshairs of Islamic fundamentalism, and we need a president who's going to keep them on defense, who's going to keep going after them and going after them.

As President Bush has told me a number of times, the idea is to kill them before they get here, and those that are here, hopefully we can get them with the Patriot Act, and that's where we have to go.

MORRIS: Yes, kill them before they get here. If we're putting 130,000 troops in Iraq, a magnet for Al Qaida terrorists, and the terrorists come from around the world, and we are able to fight them in the streets of Falujah, not in the streets of New York, and kill them with professional soldiers taking them on, not women and children who are the innocent victims of attacks, we're able to keep them on the defensive.

If they're not hopping from building to building in Falujah or Baghdad, or from cave to cave in Afghanistan and Pakistan, they're knocking down buildings in New York or smashing into buildings in Washington. And so we have a choice: do we keep them on the defense, or do we stay on the defense?

KING: There is no choice. You have to go after them. And the 9/11 families, almost every one, realize that we have to go after the Axis of Evil – it's a very, very dangerous world out there.

People say that we've alienated our allies. I think that was one of the most important things President Bush did, to make it clear that we're not going to allow second or third rate military countries such as France and Germany have a veto power over our foreign policy. When we were in Kosovo, the United States did 95 percent of the air strikes, 95 percent during the first Gulf War. Yes, there was this large alliance we had, but the United States and Britain did the fighting.

NATO itself is almost a shell, unfortunately. And the president made it clear that he was not going to allow the French to use the Security Council to have a veto power over what we're going to do militarily. In the war in Kosovo, you had 19 countries had a veto power over American air strikes, but we carried 95 percent of them. It's madness to allow Belgium to have veto power, to allow the French to have a veto power.

The president tried to get allies on our side, but once they made it clear they were resisting, he went ahead. And that was a very important doctrine and a principle to set – not to be tied down by international political correctness.

MORRIS: And when we did allow Old Europe to determine our policies in Bosnia, we had 250,000 Muslims who died as a result of those policies. What happened in Bosnia was that the British and the French sent in peace-keepers when there was no peace – and Germans and all of those countries participated. And then they were worried that if we took effective action against the Serbian invaders we would be imperiling their peacekeeper troops on the ground. They were in effect hostages to the aggressors. And the result is that we were not able to lift the arms embargo, to give the Bosnian Muslims the ability to defend themselves, and we weren't able to stop the Serbian aggression because we were handcuffed by the people on the continent. Then we finally took matters into our own hands, neglected the United Nations, and in three weeks it was ended. No more genocide, no more rapes, no more pillage – civilization returned.

With thanks to Gary Waltrip, ChronWatch

KING: I remember being in Congress in the early 1990s and having European leaders coming in and lecturing us about how uninformed we were, how simplistic we were to think there would ever be a military solution to Bosnia. And yet once we did use force, it was over in 3 weeks. We saved Europe again from what would have been such incredible crimes against humanity, and they never gave us credit. Not that we're looking for credit, but there genocide going on in their own backyard and they couldn't resolve it. And it took us three weeks.

MORRIS: There's always been an international division of labor here. The United States is equipped to be the world's policeman, when we have to be. We're the only country that really can deal with these threats. Other countries are very good at helping them govern, helping them administer themselves, helping them establish an ongoing regime, but they just don't have the military wherewithal.

And there was the same pessimism about Afghanistan. We were entering the hellhole that had destroyed the Russian army. We were going to fight in the mountains that had carved up the Red Army. We were going to be stuck in Afghanistan for decades. We were going to be hunted in the mountains by random hit and run gangs. And none of that happened.

Then when we went into Iraq. Oh, there would be germ warfare. Oh, the oil wells would erupt in flames and it would take years to extinguish the flames. Oh, the supplies would be overextended. Oh, we'd have too few troops. Oh, when we got into Baghdad the house to house fighting would keep us there forever, in a quagmire. Then after we win the war, very quickly and very efficiently, we then serve as a magnet for terrorists from all over the world who come to Iraq for their summer vacations and their purposes, to try to kill American soldiers. Well yes, that's what we want, we want them to go after our troops, not to go after our cities. And we want our troops to kill them, we want to smoke them out of the mountains, get them out of their hiding places, get them to confront us, and kill them. That's our goal, that's what we're trying to do. And thank God

140,000 brave Americans are willing to risk their lives to do that. Thank the Lord that we've been able to destroy tens of thousands of these terrorists. And does anybody think it's any coincidence that while we've been doing this, we haven't been attacked?

KING: I remember reading day after day in The New York Times about the quagmire we were in in Afghanistan. I remember having a newspaper on my desk one evening watching the news in my office in Washington, and turning to my staff and saying, Did I miss something or did we just win the war today? We won battle after battle after battle, and that war was over in 6 weeks.

MORRIS: Now people say, "Well the war's not over, we still haven't caught Osama bin Laden, we still haven't pacified Afghanistan, the place is still violent. Obviously Iraq is still violent." But let's get it straight: In April the United States lost 155 brave men and women in Iraq. In May the United States lost 64 brave men and women. In June we lost 31, in July, which was the month of the handover, we lost 44. So you know, we're getting it under control, we're taking care of that, we're stabilizing it.

There is no longer this massive regime making war, threatening its neighbors and ultimately threatening the United States, there is no longer this national base for the Al Qaida to operate in Afghanistan. If you had told the hundred people in your district who had relatives killed on 9/11 that there would be no more terrorist attacks for 3 years, what would they have thought?

KING: They wouldn't have believed it. We were expecting another one every day. And since then there's been any number of occasions -- Memorial Day, the anniversary of September 11th, the World Series, a live sporting event, political events -- we keep expecting it. It doesn't happen, and that's not an accident. Listen, an attack could still happen, but the fact is, they are on defense.

In Iraq, the president is sending a signal that it's a hotbed of Islamic fundamentalism and we are not giving a dictator the benefit of the doubt, when he refuses to account for his weapons of mass destruction. That was a signal that was sent to Qaddafi of Libya. Now think back a few years at how terrified we were of Libya. That's the first time we started putting obstacles up in Washington. Now Qaddafi voluntarily starts turning over his weapons of mass destruction.

He doesn't go to the United Nations, he goes to the British and he goes to the Americans, because he realizes we are the ones who are serious. And many of these Arab leaders that we deal with behind the scenes, are telling us we're doing the right thing. They wanted us to go into Iraq, because they knew there was no hope of stability in that region so long as Saddam Hussein was there.

MORRIS: We should listen to an authority on this subject. We should listen to Osama bin Laden. In 1993 he and the warlords in Somalia were working to defeat the United States which had sent in troops to feed the starving people in Somalia. And the United States Rangers went in, and 19 of our soldiers were killed in the famous Blackhawk down incident. And Clinton chose to run, and we never again mounted combat operations. In 1999 Osama bin Laden did an interview with Esquire magazine, where he said that he was amazed that the American troops pulled out. He said, "I concluded that the United States is a paper tiger."

So the real question in the post-9/11 era is: would the United States be willing to risk casualties? Would America be willing to see its soldiers die in an effort to fight terrorism and to protect civilization? I think that the casualties that we're experiencing in Iraq, while every one of them makes you want to bleed, every one of them also makes a statement: When you attack us you have got to realize that we will pay whatever price it is to stop you from attacking us again.

KING: You're right. As tragic as those deaths are, you multiply that by

thousands if we don't take the action. And that's the purpose of having a strong armed forces. If you realize that every sacrifice we make today is going to prevent another World Trade Center attack, prevent another Pentagon attack, that's a sacrifice the country must make.

When you are in the White House, and you're getting all that heat, it takes guts on your part to stick it out. There's other presidents who would have backed off. But the tougher it gets, the more resolute President Bush is. And that does send a signal to these countries. To me, it's no mystery why Musharraf from Pakistan is standing with us now. Right after September 11th, President Bush dealt with Musharraf. The very next day, he sent emissaries to Musharraf, telling him "are you with us or against us?" Musharraf had been playing it both ways for a long time. Pakistan got the message.

MORRIS: One of the scenes in Michael Moore's movie that is most affecting is when he looks into the eyes of a politician and says, "Would you be willing to see your son or your daughter killed in Iraq to defend Falujah?" Now you have looked into the eyes of mothers and fathers who have had their children killed in Falujah. What do they say?

KING: Most of them realize that they didn't die defending Falujah, they died defending the United States. You'll say Iwo Jima was an island which meant nothing, but in the larger sense that's how we defeated Japan. So all of these small battles are part of a large mosaic of protecting the United States against evil and against tyranny. It really demeans and diminishes the sacrifices made by our soldiers who have died in these battles when Michael Moore tries to make them sound insignificant. The fact is dying in Falujah is the same as dying for New York or dying for Washington – you're defending the United States.

MORRIS: But what do the parents say?

KING: The parents I know of, and there's been a number of them, support what the president's doing. There was one family I've spoken to that has doubts, but they don't hold it against President Bush, they just have doubts about the war itself. But none of them feel that their son died in vain or that it was wrong. Some of them are more dedicated than ever. I mean they feel if their son or daughter have done the right thing. And they're proud. They feel diminished when they see others trying to take advantage of their sons' death, by trying to trivialize it.

MORRIS: Or to use their sons' death as an excuse for giving up the fight.

KING: Exactly. I've been to Iraq, I've been to see these troops. The overwhelming majority are proud to be there. They'd all rather be home, every soldier wants to come home. But they know they're doing a good job, they're proud of what they're doing, and the resentment that I pick up from the military there, it's resentment of the media. When they see the evening news and it looks as if Iraq is in flames, when they know that at any given time, 99 percent of Iraq is stable. All the schools are open, all the hospitals are open, there is no starvation, there is no mass migration out. All of the things that were predicted didn't happen. They're proud of what they're doing, and they resent the slanted images given by the American media.

MORRIS: And the only reason their lives are at risk is that the Pentagon wants to save the lives of Iraqis. Let's start with the fact that if we want to deal with that sheik who's hiding up in that mosque. We could take care of the sheik, the whole city, in one big bang. We're not going to do that, okay. But we have a lot of other ordinance we could use. We could level that town in a matter of moments. We're not going to do that. We could drop precision guided munitions, which would only hit certain targets. But we're not going to do that, because it's a mosque and we're not going to violate a holy shrine that means a lot to people. We're not going to do that. We could send in the army, send in tanks, send in 10,000 men, overwhelm the town, shoot everything that moves, spare some of the real estate, but pacify it. We're not going do that either, because we don't want to shoot innocents. So what we are doing is asking our young men and women to go doorway to doorway to doorway, without the incredible technology that America has, and we're asking them to risk their lives, not just killing the enemy, but killing the enemy in a way that doesn't kill innocent civilians, that doesn't alienate the population at the same time. And that is why we've been incurring casualties.

KING: Yes, that is our policy. We are going very slowly, very gradually, trying to win minds and hearts, trying not to kill innocent people. When I was in Baghdad what struck me was, after all of the shock and awe and all of those bombs were dropped, there was minimal damage in Baghdad. This wasn't Berlin in 1945. This wasn't Hiroshima and Nagasaki. The military did very targeted attacks because we did not want to destroy the civilian infrastructure, we did not want to kill civilians. I mean there's probably never been more firepower used with less people killed than what we did in Baghdad.

MORRIS: I think the military has adjusted to the humanitarian and political realities of the world in which we live. Back in Vietnam, we did massive bombing, lots of innocent people killed, lots of POWs taken. But we don't want innocent people killed, so we developed precision guided munitions where the bomb hits only that target. We didn't want POWs, so we developed remotely piloted drones. And we don't want a lot of civilian casualties, so we changed our infantry tactics to a point where we save lives. That's a very important commentary on the values the United States brings into that conflict.

KING: And listen—the Iraqi people don't want an occupying power, there's going to be some resentment against us. But they don't want us to leave yet either, because they realize if we did leave the violence that could

With thanks to Cox & Forkum

be upon them. They also realize that no matter what you say about the American military, even if you take the worst the United States has ever done and put it all together, it doesn't add up to one day of the tyranny of Saddam Hussein. They know what tyranny is, they know what oppression is, they know what military brutality is, they know what executions are, and they know what it's like to live under tyranny, and they know that it's not the United States.

MORRIS: In John Kerry's acceptance speech, he said that we crossed a crucial line - that in the past we had always fought wars because we have to, and that now presumably in Iraq, we were fighting a war because we want to. Do you think that that's what we're doing in Iraq?

KING: We're fighting it because we have to. John Kerry somehow gives the impression that the United States has never gone to war before unless we've been attacked. We weren't attacked in Korea, we weren't attacked in Haiti or in Bosnia or in Kosovo. The fact is, we are in Iraq because it's in our national interest, it is in the interest of the region, and in the interest of the Iraqi people. That's why we're there. And to somehow suggest that we're there because we want to be there, that this is some kind of a frolic we're off on – to me, it demeans the country, it demeans the sacrifice, and it really demeans the purpose and the reason for why we're there.

MORRIS: Do you think that there is the remotest possibly that we would have invaded Iraq if 9/11 never happened?

KING: The main reason for attacking Iraq is to stabilize the region where there's such a large element of Islamic fundamentalists. After 9/11 we had to attack Iraq, because there was no way we can defeat Islamic fundamentalism unless we take out an unstable regime, a regime which could have provided weapons of mass destruction and assistance to Islamic fundamentalists in the region.

It would have been criminal negligence on the part of any president not to go after Iraq after 9/11. Before 9/11 you could have had a debate – should we or should we not, you know, larger diplomatic reasons. After 9/11, to me there was absolutely no excuse whatsoever.

First of all it was important to get control of the area, but also it was sending a signal to other tyrants and other dictators, and to the terrorists, that they were going to be on defense from here on in. There was a new United States, and we are fighting a war so they never come at us again.

MORRIS: We come from a heritage where Vietnam is in the minds of everybody. I was a very active participant in the anti-Vietnam war movement because the war was a mistake. The fall of Vietnam did not have anything to do with delaying the fall of the Soviet Union or the collapse of communism. And there weren't any dominoes: Thailand didn't fall, Malaysia didn't fall, Indonesia didn't fall, Philippines didn't fall – all of those nightmare scenarios turned out to be wrong. And I honor those men who died in Vietnam, I feel that so intensely. I believe they died in a mistake, not their mistake God knows, but in a mistake. But those men and women who are dying in Afghanistan, or Iraq -- that is no mistake. They are dying because we were attacked and we will be attacked again, and they are protecting their loved ones, every day and every hour that they're there. And I just pray that they understand that, Michael Moore notwithstanding.

KING: Yes, people can debate Vietnam, but when it comes to Iraq and Afghanistan there should be no hesitation at all. I mean, this is to protect America. We are under siege. We are in the crosshairs, we are the ones who are being targeted, and we have to stop it where it comes from, which is the Middle East. We also have to protect ourselves here at home, and that's why we have the Patriot Act, why we have more law enforcement, why we have more cooperation between FBI and local police and CIA.

MORRIS: When I worked for President Clinton, something always came before fighting terror. He would have imposed sanctions on companies that helped Iran develop its oil industry under the bill passed by congress that authorized it. But appeasing the western Europeans whose companies those were, came first. He would have attacked bin Laden in a kidnapping operation and snatched him, but the risk of assassination of bin Laden without a memorandum of notification authorizing it, came first. He would have fired missiles at bin Laden, but the risk of collateral damage, came first. He would have been more aggressive in dealing with Iraq, but the risk of killing civilians and innocents, came first. He would have cut off the supply of oil revenues to Saddam Hussein, but the need to try to make sure people didn't starve in Iraq, came first. Something always came first before fighting the war on terror. He would have cracked down on funding of terrorist organizations, but the concern about inadvertently hurting good organizations, came first. He would have dealt aggressively with surveillance and wire tapping to deal with terrorists, but civil liberties concerns came first. Something always came before the priority of fighting terrorism. And that environment has changed under Bush, and I'm very concerned that if Bush is defeated, we're going to go back to the time when everything else comes first.

KING: And President Bush doesn't want that to happen. He knows there's no such thing as an easy or quick victory, there's no such thing as a guaranteed win, there's no such thing as not having some blood spilled, there's no such thing as not having injustices done. There's always going to be some negative consequence from what you do. But the most horrific consequence is not to take the tough action. We never want to see September 11th again.

MORRIS: Michael Moore makes a big deal of the seven or rather five minutes after George Bush learned that there was an attack on in the United States. I consider myself fairly substantive, I think that I know public policy pretty well, I think I'm pretty good at handling political crises, but thank

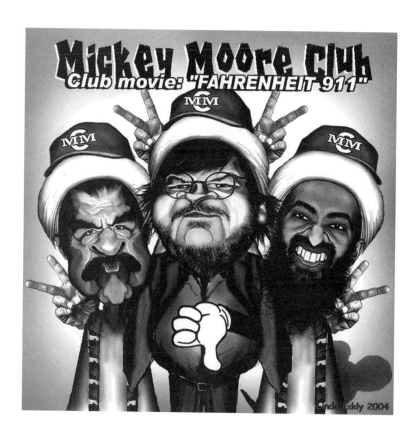

With thanks to Linda Eddy, Iowa Presidential Watch

goodness there was no camera on me for the first few minutes of that attack. Because all I did was stare with my eyes open and my mouth open at that television set. I didn't think anything, I didn't do anything, I didn't take any action. I was just letting the enormity of that absorb and wash over me.

And when we criticize George Bush, we really are asking him to be superhuman. When you're confronted with something like that, in the first few minutes, you just watch and you absorb it. And let's also understand that he's the President of the United States. He's not an emergency worker. His job is not to run the fire department or the police department. His job is to be the president.

KING: I think the president did exactly the right thing. Let's go back to what happened. Andy Card came up and told him the United States is under attack, the second tower had been hit. The staff was in the adjoining room. They were setting up contact with the White House, the Pentagon, to find out what was going on. Ari Fleischer actually held up a note saying, "Don't say anything" because the staff was trying to find out what happened. What the president did was sit there, and get his thoughts together. There was nothing he could have done at that moment. He was waiting for his staff to find out what happened. Once that was done, he got up and calmly walked out. On all accounts he was on the phone immediately with the vice president, with Condoleezza Rice, with cabinet officials, directing what had to be done, in full command.

By the way, the media was there that day. Not one person reported the president did the wrong thing. This is really reconstruction, revisionist history three years after the fact.

MORRIS: Bush was probably sitting there saying to himself, I don't want to say anything that makes more of these attacks possible. And I'm going to follow the advice of the police and military people, the security people on my staff, who understand what the situation is.

KING: Right, for all he knew there could have 15 to 20 other attacks going on. He could have been targeted there in Florida. The idea was to let people find out what was going on, and then he would respond. And you know, the American people are the best judges of this. Because certainly from September 11th and for the next 3, 4, 5 days, probably for the first time in more than 30 years, we had unscripted politics in this country. No one could write the lines for the president – he had to act on his own. And maybe he was not perfect at each stage along the way, but the American people liked what they saw. They saw a strong leader, they saw a president who was there doing what had to be done. And they're the best judges.

RON SILVER

(While driving across Manhattan)

FAHRENHYPE 9/11: What's it like living in New York after 9/11?

RON SILVER: In the back of everybody's mind is the world that we live in now, which is interesting, because in New York, living with a certain amount of terror is part of your birthright. You have to depend on trusting and the kindness of other strangers. You get into the subway and you don't know who's in the subway that day. You're walking along streets and passing people, you're in elevators with people, you depend on people to drive you here and there all the time. So there's a certain trust and a certain community that we're all in this together. And now there's a certain uncertainty. Everything is fraught with caution now.

FAHRENHYPE 9/11: Wasn't there just another threat?

SILVER: Yes, they arrested a couple of men that were looking to bomb the D train. Now you can't shut down the subway system, and it's almost impossible to secure it.

FAHRENHYPE 9/11: But nobody seems to take these threats seriously anymore -- why?

SILVER: I believe it stems from the dissipation of feelings about 9/11. Europe and many parts of the world have realized that they are not the primary targets. That dissipated a lot of it. I think a lot of people resent America when it responds forcefully and uses its might, whether it's cultural, economic, diplomatic or military, to respond to a situation when our own security's involved. They like the use of American power in the world for humanitarian reasons, if it's used to do good, if it's used to protect other people, but in response to our own security needs, there's a large segment

of population that almost reflexively recoils from using power in defense of ourselves.

FAHRENHYPE 9/11: Are you describing Michael Moore?

SILVER: I'm not in the habit of rooting against America, and that seems to be Michael Moore's core principle, regardless of where he goes in the world. He calls Americans dumb. He talked about the epicenters of evil in the world, he said that "Israel, the oil companies, Halliburton—it's all the same ball of wax." I'm not a fan of that kind of analysis.

He's a movie maker that can manipulate images. You give me enough footage on a subject, and I can put together a film and have you believe anything I want. It all depends how you put it together, the use of truths and half truths. He's a clown. People seem to enjoy the film. Let them enjoy it. I hope they don't take any political lessons away from it. That would be a shame.

FAHRENHYPE 9/11: Can you give us an example of how Michael Moore manipulated images?

SILVER: I didn't find a single frame that was honest. Take the way he put the 2000 election together. All the analyses afterwards with CNN, with the *Washington Post*, with everybody, said that Bush would have won the election regardless of how small the margin was. And any injustices that may or may not have happened were actually on the other side, because the networks made calls that Gore won Florida before the panhandle was closed. That's a Republican area, and some people have estimated that 10,000 Bush voters did not even stand on line or go to the polls because they thought the election was already done.

You see footage, and you assume that it's victory footage. You assume that Gore had won and that they're celebrating. And Ben Affleck was there and Stevie Wonder, and the music was going, and they had the banner up.

And Moore makes it seem like this all had to be withdrawn, this all had to be taken back after the shenanigans supposedly went on. What he failed to mention is, that footage was of a rally from before and it was not a celebration party.

The whole movie is rife with that stuff. I think *Fahrenheit 9/11* will be thought of as "Reefer Madness" kind of kitschy film. For my taste, Joseph Goebbels was a much better propagandist. I like Leni Riefenstahl as a filmmaker much more. Ezra Pound was far more lyrical during the Second World War. And I understand Tokyo Rose was more attractive.

FAHRENHYPE 9/11: As we've driven through the neighborhoods that you grew up in, you've talked about a new kind of civility since 9/11, but there seems to be no such civility in the political debate?

SILVER: Michael Moore is divisive. He pretends to be a representative of the people, a tribune of the people, one with the people. Nothing is further from the truth. His scorn, his disdain for poor, uneducated people comes through in almost everything he does. His humiliating people – the trap he set for Charlton Heston in Bowling for Columbine – the guy has onset senile dementia – and Moore makes it seem like they were talking one week after the Columbine tragedy. It wasn't, it was a year later. He doesn't mention things like that. He's just at base, a dishonest man.

He doesn't seem to understand that one of the reasons Europeans like him is because he represents everything they find disdainful and contemptible about America. He's overweight, he's slovenly, with a baseball cap, he's unshaven – European's ideal American hero. He says what they think in their heart – "American perfidy and American hegemony and power creates pain all over the world. We don't liberate anybody, we don't do any good, we ruin everything for everybody." That's what they like to think and they love Michael for saying it.

He should apologize to the American people about what he's said, about how dumb we are. He's really a stain on America, on its values.

FAHRENHYPE 9/11:   Fine, that's his opinion, but what harm is a man spouting his opinions?

SILVER: He trivializes the threat to this country, and that's dangerous. Now if he doesn't call it a documentary – and I think on one or two occasions he's said it's a comedy – then I think anything's allowed. If it's a work of art, I think everything's allowed. There is nothing that is not permissible. But if he people call it a documentary, then there are certain parameters, certain rules of a documentary that he needs to pay attention to, and he's violated just about every principle. If he's making a spoof or a piece of satire, then I think it's perfectly acceptable what he's done, but not if he calls it a documentary.

In fact, I have a suggestion for him. If he would like to be a documentarian, he might want to go into some of the mosques in this country and talk to imams, or spend time in Hezbollah and Hamas training camps, and film how they teach their children to blow themselves up and become martyrs. He can go see how they rape and kill women. There's all sorts of things he could do as a documentarian, but he doesn't seem to be interested in that.

FAHRENHYPE 9/11: But he makes people laugh?

SILVER: There is some funny stuff in *Fahrenheit 9/11*. He got a lot of mileage out of the president reading My Pet Goat. But seriously, thank god he didn't jump up and scare everyone. Personally, I'm very interested in how Franklin Roosevelt responded on December 7th when he was told that our fleet went down at Pearl Harbor. How did he respond? Did he sit there for 10 minutes thoughtfully, asking himself "how do we respond to this?" I liked what the president projected.

If Michael Moore is willing to read into the president's mind, then I'm

"I told them I wanted the best clown and the best illusionist money could buy."

With thanks to Juju Dandridge Suits

willing to read into the president's mind in saying, "okay, we don't have enough information yet, I'm not going to scare these kids. There are a lot of cameras on me right now. I'll stay here and in an acceptable time go outside and deal with what I have. I thought it was very adult, calm projection of leadership. Michael Moore saw something else in his eyes. So you see what you want to see. But given the aftermath of that day, we know his response was very measured.

I've read both Woodward books. I don't think Michael Moore has read one. I'm finishing the 9/11 commission report. A lot of how he responded to it was truly courageous, rigorous leadership. It's been consistent. And most important, the enemy knows it. That's what's terribly important, because a lot of people mistake honesty for arrogance. A lot of people mistake consistency for rigidity. A lot of people mistake clarity for simplicity. And a lot of people mistake courage for stupidity. I don't. It took us two to three weeks to identify the source, in Afghanistan. And unlike Michael and other people who said we should have gone in with overwhelming force, I think Bush understood from the Russian experience in Afghanistan that there was a better way to do it.

FAHRENHYPE 9/11: Have the media given Michael Moore a free ride, choosing not to point out how obviously flawed his movie is?

SILVER: I think there was a collusion between a lot of the media that felt as Moore felt, and wanted to elevate this into something it wasn't. Plain fact is, the film is a Saturday Night Live sketch. Some parts are done well. There's some laughs in the thing. Some are disgraceful and repugnant. Happy Iraqis flying balloons and getting haircuts – it's a disgraceful cut. He's wrong on the information about Bush being on vacation. Look, he obviously feels very guilty for helping elect Bush, because he supported Nader in 2000. So I understand the psychological thing, but given his politics he should be supporting Nader again, instead of getting down on his knees on a TV show begging Nader not to run.

If Moore believes in democracy, you don't try to keep a candidate off the ballot. If Moore was honest with himself, he'd back Nader again because Nader's the true alternative. Because John Kerry, God bless him, has a position very close to Bush on Iraq. He's a responsible, honorable man. He's not gonna butcher the troops, notwithstanding what most of his party wants to do. So if Moore wanted to do a public service he would build a third party that really agrees with him that America is perfidious, that we're a danger to the world, that corporations are invidiously harming poor people all over the world. Nader's his guy – get rid of the duopoly.

FAHRENHYPE 9/11: You speak of other political issues—

SILVER: The central issue of our times is terror, and terrorist groups having access to weapons of mass destruction. There is no other issue in this election for me, and I don't think there should be for anybody. The threat is too catastrophic to even contemplate. And if we're wrong, if we don't do it right, the costs are incalculable, and history will not forgive us.

Michael Moore is mistaken about a lot of things. He misunderstands the administration is trying to protect us. Misunderstands what's good about the Patriot Act. Misunderstands history. When history looks back on this period, Michael Moore and that faction of the party are in danger of being seen as Charles Lindbergh and the isolationists and the America Firsters who in 1937 and 1938 said, It doesn't make any sense to go to war, Germany has a legitimate grievance from World War I, and eight years later in 1945, they wished to God they had gone to war and stopped Germany in '37.

Bush chose not to be surprised by the inevitable. Bush chose to stop them because it's only a matter of time before there's a nuclear weapon used on a major city with millions of people. If it never happens, great. But the odds have run too high. I'm not trusting myself or my children's safety, or our nation's safety in the hands of Michael Moore's perspective on how to protect us. I think they're in danger of being horribly wrong when the history books are written.

FAHRENHYPE 9/11: You used to study foreign policy, correct? What do you think about Moore's portrayal of the U.S.-Saudi relationship?

SILVER: The relationship with Saudi Arabia goes back to Roosevelt – there are pictures of every American president with Saudis since and why wouldn't there be, given the course of history? They've given millions of dollars to every president, including President Clinton for his library.

Moore segues artlessly from the Saudis to the Carlyle Group, suggesting that all these Republicans are enriching themselves from their secretive group. It's mostly Democrats in the Carlyle Group. And here's a doozy of a conspiracy theory for you: Carlyle has a stake in the Lowe's Theater Chain. I wonder if any of Michael's films ever played there, and if so it means Michael has a nefarious tie to Carlyle. Come on!

Then Michael suggests that Bush spirited some Saudi families out right after 9/11 when there was a no-fly order in place. Turns out a mid-level staffer named Richard Clarke gave the order, not Bush. And guess why they wanted to leave? Nineteen Saudis killed 2900 people in New York, I'd be on a plane tomorrow, whether I had anything to do with it or not. Of course they wanted to go.

Unlike Michael Moore, I don't think George Bush is an illegitimately installed, dumb fascist who is leading America down a spider hole because of his corporate interests, and he wants to make more money for oil companies. That's Michael Moore's position. That's fine. That's not mine. Maybe I'm not as sophisticated a political observer as he is.

I actually trust the president. This may shock some people, but I think this is a man of faith. I think on 9/11 he felt that he needed to do something to protect the American people. I think going on the offense is the appropriate response in this world.

FAHRENHYPE 9/11: Having said that, was the post-war planning for Iraq

With thanks to Mike Lester, The Rome News-Tribune

good?

SILVER: No, it was wretched. Been surprised by a long of things, didn't plan for a lot of things, and the learning curve has been very steep. But I think we're headed in the right direction. And contrary to conventional wisdom, the president's been very flexible, and when he sees something doesn't work, he's willing to make the change. They've made lots of mistakes, but that's the nature of fighting a war.

FAHRENHYPE 9/11: How would today's media have treated the Second World War?

SILVER: In early 1942, we had 760 sailors go down off the coast of England in an accident. 760 went down. Can you imagine what the media would have done with that? The war in the Pacific -- you want to talk quagmire, you want to talk about giving up, about the wrong decision.

Sometimes there's two sides to an issue, sometimes not. So if you went back and voraciously read the papers in the Iraq war, you'd read about every day there was a quagmire in Baghdad...before it fell in three weeks. Every day the Marines stopped for 48 hours because of a sandstorm...are we bogged down? Is it another Vietnam? There's a whole industry out there now.

FAHRENHYPE 9/11: Why is the Democratic Party treating Michael Moore like a serious policy wonk?

SILVER: If they'd dismiss him, fine. But at the D.C. opening of *Fahrenheit 9/11*, the party chairman Terry McCauliff hailed the movie. Senators' Hawkins, Boxer and Daschle were there, Henry Waxman was there. So you had the Democratic leadership embracing the commercial film with so many – to be kind – flaws. It degrades the political conversation. Because if the Democratic Party – of which I'm a member – finds that film accept-able, we're even more unhinged from reality in our political campaigns. So I was very, very disappointed.

FAHRENHYPE 9/11: How have we in just three years lost the central focus on how important it is to confront terrorism?

SILVER: This is not simply a gang of thugs. We have an ideological enemy. And if people think back to the end of the Second World War, we were enervated as a nation. We were damaged. Much of our sense of security was destroyed at the time. We had to start building again. This country was not ready to embark on an ideological war for 50 years. But Harry Truman and George Kennan and Dean Atchison architected this new world, and understood that whether we like it or not, it was life or death for us. And they had to bring along the population, to understand what communism was, and what the nature of the new paradigm and the new world was going to be, which was this ideological fight against commu-nism. And it did not make Harry Truman very popular, and he took us into a war in Korea, the consequences of which we're still understanding. But however in 1989 that wall did come down in Berlin, and communism ceas-es to be a threat.

We have something similar going on now, and let's call it what it is – it's Islamic fanaticism. Now, if it was fanaticism among 100 or 200 or 1000 or 2000 people, that's one thing. But the Arab Muslim world goes along a whole arc. They have a very unhappy encounter with modernity, and we are the hegemon, the enemy. And they will do everything in their power to destroy us. And there's a tremendous amount of sympathizers in the world. They are taught from the time they're children to blame all of their ills on us. And some of them may be legitimate, but only some.

FAHRENHYPE 9/11: You studied Islam and Arab culture in graduate school—

SILVER: And I have a tremendous amount of respect for high Arab culture, and I never lose fact that a lot of Western knowledge was retained and saved because of Arabic scholars, and their high points in Spain and in Turkey, and in India. The Mogul architecture in India is some of the highest points in civilization. But that was when they were tolerant, when they understood that they needed a diverse group of people within their arc. And I look forward to that renaissance, but they're not going to do it like this.

We're going to have to do the same thing that Woodrow Wilson thought needed to be done. We're gonna have to do the same thing that Franklin D. Roosevelt was forced to do, what Harry Truman did, what John Kennedy did, and Ronald Reagan did. And whether Moore likes it or not or whether he is blinded by his rage and his vitriolic hatred for this man, this man is our leader right now, and he is responding in the way of those other presidents. When we look back in history, we'll be thankful for his response, even though they can't see it now. And I think we're very lucky to have this kind of clarity, courage, leadership in moving forward.

With thanks to Jeff Parker, Florida Today

STEVE EMERSON

FAHRENHYPE 9/11: We're speaking with one of America's foremost authorities on terrorism, Steven Emerson. He's the author of American Jihad and director of The Investigative Project. And he came to this game in the most unlikely way—

STEVEN EMERSON: I had been a correspondent at CNN and in December of 1992 was sent to Oklahoma City to cover some type of event. I found myself with some down time on Christmas day in 1992 and I went downtown looking for a fast food restaurant. And lo and behold, I discovered a whole bunch of people exiting from the Convention Center, dressed in Middle Eastern garb – long robes, head scarves. It seemed incongruous – Middle Easterners in the heart of the United States. I went inside and discovered that there was a Islamic religious convention held under the auspices of a group I had never heard of, the Muslim Arab Youth Association, which turned out to be a front group for Islamic extremists connected to Hamas and Al Qaida.

In fact, there were thousands of people attending, and scores of stalls and booths representing almost every radical Islamic group in the world. In addition, there were speakers from outside the United States, calling for jihad, death to the Jews, death to the infidels, in language that was absolutely unprecedented.

Yet when I went back to Washington and tried to get CNN and the Washington Post interested in the story, I was told that what I had witnessed didn't happen. Several weeks later, the first World Trade Center bombing occurred. CNN asked me to do a one hour special on the roots of the bombing. I returned to them with a proposal several weeks later, suggesting we look at the organizations in the United States that had developed tentacles, all the radical Islamic organizations hiding under a false veneer. And CNN's reaction was quite swift; it was too "politically sensitive."

I didn't think that should have been a criteria for what appears on TV. But for CNN it was, and I dare say continues to be to this day. I ended up leaving CNN, and ultimately got financing from the Corporation of Public Broadcasting. And ultimately I did a documentary that aired in November of '94 called Jihad in America. The documentary showed incontrovertible images – videos taken by either Islamic terrorists themselves, or undercover by people that work for me, of radical officials calling for jihad, training.

Interestingly, the reaction from some of the media's intelligentsia like the New York Times and the Washington Post was to discount any type of threat, because there was clearly no problem. That was the mentality that prevailed before 9/11, contributing to the successful deception perpetrated by the Islamic extremists, which is to hide under false veneer, claim that they're Democrat with small d, that they're liberal pluralists, when in fact they seek to cover over Islamic terrorist strikes. And they know exactly how to play the victim card, engendering sympathy and even a removal from scrutiny by the media.

FAHRENHYPE 9/11: How did this reporting effect you personally?

EMERSON: I was forced to leave my co-op in Washington in 1995 because of a threat that was conveyed to me by law enforcement. And I did, and have lived under a false cover ever since. It's not something that I worry about every day, but it's obviously an issue, insofar as the threat of militant Islam is not just the actual act of carrying out violence, it's the chilling effect of people being intimidated or afraid to talk about things. Or, it's the successful intimidation.

Hollywood has been overwhelmingly intimidated, wittingly and unwittingly, by Islamic extremists. Before 9/11, and after 9/11. Paramount Studios changed the plot line of the movie The Sum of All Fears which had in Tom Clancy's story an Islamic extremist protagonist who detonated a nuclear bomb. But Paramount changed the protagonists to right wing extremists. Why? Because various Islamic groups protested that this would be "stereotyping Muslims." That deliberate decision by Paramount is part of the problem we face, with people in positions of trust and influence willingly changing the vocabulary in order to protect the bad guys.

FAHRENHYPE 9/11: What about with the serious media?

EMERSON: Notice the reaction of The New York Times this year when it announced that it had erred in its pre-Iraq war coverage and said that it was not skeptical enough, and it had this very introspective self-criticism. Why was there no self-criticism of their coverage of the militant Islam threat?

In fact, probably the primary reason that 9/11 happened was because of one word: deception. The ability of the bad guys to hide in the United States, the fear of profiling, the fear of antagonizing "Muslim group", the fear of "stereotyping." Unfortunately, Hollywood hasn't recognized that, the New York Times has not recognized that, the Washington Post has not recognized that. Lest I be accused of generalizing – there are some good reporters at both papers. Unfortunately they are in a minority. And the reality is that this unwillingness to scrutinize the actual activities of militant Islamic groups who feign pluralism or who feign moderation is shameful and downright dangerous.

I don't tell anyone that espousing death to America should be considered illegal – that's free speech. But it shouldn't be immune from scrutiny or criticism. And Hollywood is afraid to touch it. The only bad guys they can touch are people in the U.S. government or people on the right wing.

FAHRENHYPE 9/11: What has caused this moral blindness?

EMERSON: The fact is, Islamic groups have been able to prevail with their deception in ways that would only be considered farcical if David Duke were able to get away with representing himself as a civil rights organization. He would never get to first base.

With thanks to Cox & Forkum

In Europe, there are lots of left wing intellectuals who understand the threat of militant Islam. In Turkey, in the Muslim world, there are women's groups who understand the threat of militant Islam, who understand what happens to women when they're quote "guilty of an honor crime." They see it firsthand. And in this country, there has been this moral blindness that perhaps was understandable before 9/11, but in the 3 years since, I find myself unable to explain what governs this myopia.

FAHRENHYPE 9/11: Why is it so hard to make people understand that there's a real threat?

EMERSON: Before 9/11, I struggled for years to investigate, expose, combat the rise and proliferation of Islamic extremists. And in reality I failed. It took the deaths of 3000 people for us to get concerned as a nation. The only thing that I was able to do was essentially chronicle and collect intelligence on what the bad guys were doing. Fortunately, there are people within the U.S. government that understand this. The only time people get upset is when they feel there's a threat. All politics is local, all terrorism is local. The question is, how do people feel the threat today, if there aren't bombs going off?

FAHRENHYPE 9/11: Michael Moore has been linked to terrorist organizations – is that a fair characterization?

EMERSON: I find it an irony that Michael Moore is so self-righteous and indignant about the fact that the Saudis allegedly were allowed to leave the United States after 9/11. Here's a guy that speaks before groups that have justified Islamic terrorism, that are part of the Islamic fundamentalist agenda, that deny rights to women, that espouse and rationalize terrorist violence against Jews and Christians, that in fact are part and parcel of the entire Saudi Wahhabist agenda. And he speaks before these groups as if they're the equivalent of the Rotary Club.

I suggest that Michael Moore has legitimized groups that have the moral stain of blood on their hands. And insofar as Michael Moore is a man who pretends to be a great moral arbiter, I think someone has to ask him why he would speak before groups that have justified the use of violence and terrorism against Jews, Christians and others.

FAHRENHYPE 9/11: What proof of this do you have?

EMERSON: I have a tape of the head of The Muslim Brotherhood openly saying that Islam will reign supreme throughout the world, will reconquer Europe, reconquer. Speaking to Islamic groups in Ohio. And in fact his agenda was clearly there for us to see. It was a 1995 speech. I have it on videotape. And he also says Islam will take over the United States.

I have footage of Michael Moore's speech when he received an award from the Muslim Public Affairs Committee in Los Angeles in October of 2003. He lavishly praised this group, a group which has rationalized the killing of Americans in Beirut, and on its website has refused to condemn Hezbollah or Hamas, or even the issue of Saudi Wahhabism.

I dare say that if a Republican Party official spoke before the Institute for Historical Revisionism, a Holocaust denial group, or before a David Duke convention, the event would be widely criticized. But to the extent that Michael Moore and others have spoken before these terror-supporting groups and legitimized them, I think this is a clear and present danger to our national security. This is the reason why 9/11 happened.

FAHRENHYPE 9/11: Osama bin Laden is a figurehead at this point—

EMERSON: Anybody who focuses only on the threat posed by Osama or Al Qaida is in denial or misleading the American public. The larger threat is of Islamic extremism. Period.

I honestly do not know how smart people can mistake the enemy so blatantly, and portray President Bush somehow as more insidious and evil than Osama bin Laden or Islamic extremism. I suppose one could draw parallels to other periods in American history, when either those that thought that Nazi Party was really a friendly party, or that communists were really our friends. One doesn't have to be a right wing ideologue to understand the threat here. The threat comes from people who would deny us the very values that have made this country so free: pluralism, separation of church and state. And yet I find it amazing that there are people like Michael Moore who would defend those groups that want to end the separation of church and state. Maybe anthropologists a thousand years from now will be able to figure out the DNA of people so morally blinded to this clear and present danger.

FAHRENHYPE 9/11: Why hasn't there been a post-9/11 wave of attacks like so many people expected?

EMERSON: It's attributable to one of several factors. 1) Either good luck, or 2) the fact that a lot of them are taking early retirements, or 3) they simply haven't been able to reconstitute their networks, or 4) they're preoccupied with surpassing previous levels of attack so they want to do something much more spectacular.

What I fear is not an attack in 2004. I fear there isn't going to be an attack in 2004, 2005, or 2006 or 2007. And you can be sure at the end of those three or four years, there will be votes in Congress to terminate counter-terrorist programs. There will be the unraveling entirely of any type of anti-terrorist legislation. And that's when the bad guys will strike, and then we'll simply re-repeat history with another commission to say, "Why didn't we get it right?" Now here in the aftermath of 9/11, there's an opportunity to get it right.

Now it's not Norwegian women in wheelchairs that are striking us in the heart of Manhattan. It's Islamic extremists, and it's their Islamic vision of

With thanks to Mike Lester, The Rome News-Tribune

hegemony. That doesn't mean all Muslims are part of a terrorist conspiracy, it doesn't mean that all Muslims are extremists. But the reality is that
the central gravity of Islamic institutions today – the media, in the religious
spheres, in the governments, in the political spheres – is mired in the
Islamic fundamentalist agenda. That's something we don't want to accept.
After all, if we see ourselves as a tolerant society, everybody else has to be
tolerant. I call it the Kumbaya Culture – let's get around the campfire, toast
some marshmallows, and we'll all go home happy. Doesn't work that way.

FAHREHYPE 9/11: How effective has U.S. counter-terrorism been post 9/11?

EMERSON: The country has seen some incredibly dedicated prosecutions
unfold when prior to 9/11 they have been able to get away with murder.
The head of Islamic jihad in the United States, a professor at the University
of South Florida who had been immune from prosecution, was indicted in
a major series of counts for murder in 2003.

The Hamas organization doesn't go by Hamas in the U.S. They go by
such nice names as the Holy Land Foundation for Relief and Development.
And they go by the Islamic Association for Palestine. But fortunately, due
to the incredibly hard work of prosecutors and FBI agents, leaders of those
groups have been indicted. Since 9/11, we have seen Islamic "charities"
shut down, because they were fronts for bin Laden or other Islamic extremists.

There have been cells exposed in upstate New York, New York City,
Chicago, Tampa, Detroit, San Diego, Los Angeles, Denver, Tulsa – not all
necessarily showing the stereotypical characteristics of a terrorist organization, but all having connections to terrorist organizations. The reality is that
they have embedded themselves in the United States. What better place to
do it than the U.S.?

Why did bin Laden send people into the United States to live here, to
train here? He could have sent people in 3 days before 9/11, he could have
practiced overseas in taking over planes. He knew they would get away far
more with their ability to hide and train and acquire the expertise in the

heart of the great Satan than anyplace else, because we're such a soft society.

FAHRENHYPE 9/11: What kind of message does Michael Moore's film send?

EMERSON: It sends a message that somehow George Bush or the U.S. government is the incarnation of evil and that only emboldens Islamic groups and Islamic terrorists to believe that somehow there is a major successful effort that they have been able to launch in the United States to divide the U.S. population, and therefore their acts of violence have actually achieved success, which is to change U.S. policy, and foist some type of internal division.

We witnessed it at the Democratic convention. One of the biggest applause lines was to Barack Obama when he alleged that Arab Americans were being rounded up off the street in the United States. This type of demagoguery creates an impression that somehow the U.S. is engaged in a war against Islam. There's no such thing. We have bent over backwards.

After 9/11, the question we asked is "what did we do?" The question is not what did we do or why do they hate us. It's "why hasn't there been any type of reciprocal response of self-criticism, of a Saudi 9/11 commission, or any effort to admit culpability on the part of Islamic extremists?" None whatsoever. It's all "we have nothing to do with it" or "this doesn't represent Islam." Well I'm willing to accept that the vast majority of Muslims do condemn terrorism. But from the leaders there has been almost no voices raised saying "we have a problem in terms of Islamic extremism.

FAHRENHYPE 9/11: Are we seeing the consensus over the Patriot Act dissolve?

EMERSON: If you ask most Americans, "should the FBI have the right to read your library card" eight in ten say no. If you ask them, "suppose a Islamic militant from Pakistan goes into the New York City library and checks out books on anthrax and mustard gas, should the FBI read it?" they say "not only should they have the right, they should be obligated to read it." So there's a disconnect here.

When I hear people say, "George Bush should go after the terrorists, not Muslims" I say, "what planet are these people on?" It's not like terrorists wear hats saying I'm a terrorist, differentiate me from the vast majority of Muslims. They hide under that deception. And unless the Islamic community disgorges them, it's up to the FBI, Department of Justice, and Homeland Security to identify who represents a threat to us.

CHAPTER 4

IF FAHRENHYPE 9/11 HAD BEEN A FICTIONAL SPOOF LIKE FAHRENHEIT 9/11

FROM the beginning, we decided not to play on Michael's field, but on our own. That meant rising above a lot of muck and goo. No cheap shots, no fabrications, nothing but an honest telling of the truth. It meant tossing aside some of our favorite material, including this little half-developed piece about some of Michael's biggest fans...

Like Sean Penn.

Sean's a pretty talented actor and student of the human condition. So he did what any of us would do when he had something political to say, he took out a full-page ad in the *New York Times* and he dissed the President seven ways to Sunday and he made it clear that "I do not believe in a simplistic and inflammatory view of good and evil."

Well, Sean, here's how it goes. Mother Teresa good, Jack the Ripper evil. Churchill good, Hitler evil. Bush and Kerry good, Saddam and bin Laden evil.

If there's anybody who understands Michael and the real agenda he's pursuing, it's the men and women laboring in the trenches of today's film industry.

"The government itself is running exactly like the Sopranos… going to kill a lot of innocent people." – George Clooney

"The real reason we are invading Iraq now…oil" – Barbra Streisand

"This war is about…hegemony, money, power, and oil." --Dustin Hoffman

"I'm ashamed to come from the United States." --Jessica Lange

"George W. Bush is like a bad comic working the crowd, a moron." Martin Sheen, who plays a strong smart president on West Wing, because he can remember the lines he's told to read.

Today you can almost hear Hollywood's finest recording a new version of Yankee Doodle Dandy

I'm a groovy airhead liberal
Airhead liberal 'til I die
A real big heart but a head of ham
Time to go and beautify.

Yes, they really know how to entertain us. Novelist Tom Robbins called the U.S. an "adolescent bully, a pubescent punk…good to have our butts kicked." Film director Robert Altman was so turned off by America's retaliation after losing 3,000 people that he said "when I see an American flag flying, it's a joke." Novelist Gore Vidal called 9/11 a just payback for our attacks on other nations. That sage Woody Harrelson weighed in with "There can be no more deaths, no transfusions of blood for oil." Singer Bonnie Raitt added that the U.S. is "hellbent on protecting access to Iraqi oil and seems willing to risk the lives of thousands…to keep gas guzzling SUVs on the highway."

Really? If our nation is so hellbent on getting cheap oil, answer me this:

1. Why do we spend so much political and financial capital defending Israel   (which has no oil) against the Arab states (which are swimming in oil)?

With thanks to Mike Lester, The Rome News-Tribune

2. Why did we slap an oil embargo on Iraq while Saddam was still in power?

3. Why do we keep going to the United Nations and trying to convince the rest of the world to stop buying Iraqi oil?

4. Why do we blast the French and Russians who actively propped up Saddam's corrupt regime in return for oil bribes?

5. Why do we boycott oil sales from Iran, while Europeans buy all they can?

The hard fact is – Iraq produces in the neighborhood of two million barrels of oil a day, against a global oil output of 76 million barrels. So are we to believe that the war on terror is being fought over 3% of the world's oil production? It just doesn't add up.

It's a fun place, Hollywood. Lots of beautiful people telling each other how beautiful they are, and just about everyone painting in gentle liberal hues. But as Dick Morris writes, celebrity is not cerebral. And there is a startling intolerance infecting Hollywood. That Michael Moore would be emboldened to give his Bush-bashing speech at the Academy Awards is evidence that he felt comfortable amid confederates. But it goes deeper than just some award winner spouting his opinion. It's almost a form of social McCarthyism, an intolerance, a dismissal of others' points of view. And it's a shame because it bears upon the credibility of a great many sensible-minded people in the movie industry.

So to all the beautiful people in Hollywood who mouth somebody else's words, or write songs like "War, what's it good for -- absolutely nothing" or take out ads arguing moral equivalence, know that you touch a deep chord in all who yearn for peace, but know too that you are out of touch with one important reality: While you sing your sweet songs, we have Islamic fascists singing of jihad and attacking Americans and glorifying the day that "American bodies will pile up in bags." That's a problem for a lot of us. That's why good and sensible people want this President to take this war far from America's shore. That isn't some cheap song lyric, that's protecting America.

CHAPTER 5

A SELECTION FROM MICHAEL MOORE IS A BIG FAT STUPID WHITE MAN

UNTIL the movie *FahrenHYPE 9/11* came out, the rebuttals to Michael Moore consisted mostly of books and papers. Perhaps the most entertaining book was *Michael Moore Is A Big Fat Stupid White Man*. And we were fortunate to feature its authors in our movie. We've selected a particularly witty chapter from their book, and excerpted it here. Should you want the rest of their story, we highly recommend picking up their book.

In a chapter titled "And the Oscar For Acting Out Goes To..." the authors perform a little psychological analysis of Moore and conclude that he suffers from an acute case of Narcissist Personality Disorder which manifests itself in nine patterns of aberrant behavior...

1. HAS A GRANDIOSE SENSE OF SELF-IMPORTANCE

That's our boy! The only fellow (apart from prophets and evangelists) who has written a chapter in the almighty voice of God (Chapter 6 of *Dude, Where's My Country?* begins: "Hi. God here.").

As Dr. Sam Vaknin notes in his book *Malignant Self Love: Narcissism Revisited*, "The narcissist never talks—he lectures." Moore was even unable to receive an Academy Award without delivering a lecture! Typically, on receipt of such a prestigious award, the honoree welcomes the opportunity to thank those who made his work possible. But gratitude runs directly counter to the narcissist's feelings of entitlement: The contributions of others are only what Moore deserves. Why share the glory by rewarding that which deserves no reward?

2. IS PREOCCUPIED WITH FANTASIES OF UNLIMITED SUCCESS, POWER...

That's Mike, again. In the 2000 elections, he backed Nader and then bragged to the world that Gore's campaign was begging him to abandon Nader and save them from disaster. In Moore's open letter to Gore, he chastises the former vice president: "Look, Al, you have screwed up—big time. . . And now your people are calling ME, asking ME to do the job YOU'VE failed to do! Jeez, I've got enough on my plate these days, between work and the holidays coming up and the leaves I should be raking—and now I'm supposed to save YOU? Unbelievable!"

It's unbelievable, alright.

Never mind that Moore didn't seem particularly important to anyone during the presidential election cycle of 2000. When Moore tried to reach Nader on the telephone, he wound up talking to staffers, with, at most, the hope that the candidate was silently listening in. Note to Mike: If anyone really thinks you can carry a key state for them, they don't let staffers field your call; and if they are on the line, they aren't silent. Candidates, of all people, know what to kiss and when. If a fellow can deliver Michigan to them or for that matter Idaho or Delaware, they grab the phone and pucker up.

And of course there are Moore's other grandiose plans. He joined the NRA so that he could have his supporters elect him as president of the organization—a campaign that would merely require 5 million or so Moorites to become life members, at a cost of $750 each, and then cast a vote for him. (First things first, Moore should have checked out the process by which the NRA's president is elected—the vote is cast by the board of directors, not the organization's members.)

3. BELIEVES THAT HE OR SHE IS "SPECIAL" AND UNIQUE AND CAN ONLY BE UNDERSTOOD BY (OR ASSOCIATE WITH) OTHER "SPECIAL" OR UNIQUE OR

With thanks to Cox & Forkum

HIGH-STATUS PEOPLE (OR INSTITUTIONS)

It is doubtful that anyone in the history of the human race has written as many "Open Letters" to major figures (George W. Bush, Al Gore, and Yasser Arafat come to mind). Where other authors might use an open letter to appeal to the recipient's better nature and encourage change, Moore's letters almost invariably berate and heckle his recipients, treating them as his inferiors.

An amusing insight: Dr. Vaknin points out that the narcissist often expects and feels entitled "to talk directly to authority figures (and not their assistants or secretaries)." And the plot of *Roger & Me* was . . .

4. REQUIRES EXCESSIVE ADMIRATION

For all his ego and mendacity, Moore is *immensely* popular. He's got an Oscar, more film awards than we can easily count, and a following whose blind loyalty resembles that of a cult. Like cults, the Moore movement shares the drive to recruit converts (we are informed that at least one university has made *Bowling* required viewing for all Freshman English students, and elsewhere many teachers have done the same on their own). The Moore Phenomenon is certainly widespread. And as we've seen over and over again, almost everyone who dares to "not excessively admire" Moore is attacked personally and viciously.

5. HAS A SENSE OF ENTITLEMENT, I.E., UNREASONABLE EXPECTATIONS OF ESPECIALLY FAVORABLE TREATMENT OR AUTOMATIC AND FULL COMPLIANCE WITH HIS OR HER EXPECTATIONS

Douglass Urbanski, his former Hollywood manager, told the Times of London how Moore was the only client he fired in writing. "Michael Moore would never withstand the scrutiny he lays on other people," Urbanski said.

One of Moore's employees at *TV Nation* was more blunt. "For the preservation of my own soul, I have to consider him as just an entertainer," he explained, "because otherwise he's a huge asshole. If you consider him an entertainer, then his acting like a selfish, self-absorbed, pouty, deeply conflicted, easily wounded child is run-of-the-mill, standard behavior. But if he's a political force, then he's a jerk and a hypocrite. . . ."

Another example, drawn from the *New York Post*: during a speaking engagement at London's Roundhouse Theater, a petulant Moore launched into a tirade against the staff. He "stormed around all day screaming at everyone, even the 5 pound-an-hour bar staff, telling them how we were all con men and useless. Then he went on stage and did it in public." Moore apologized only after the staff essentially boycotted him, refusing even to open the doors.

6. IS "INTERPERSONALLY EXPLOITATIVE," THAT IS, USES OTHERS TO ACHIEVE HIS OR HER OWN ENDS

This is Moore, again, to a T. Daniel Radosh summed it up in his 1997 *Salon* article: "Michael Moore is phenomenally good at one thing: Getting people to make idiots of themselves on camera."

Moore's movies are littered with people he talks into an interview and then exploits, portraying them as crass or ignorant and using them to highlight his own superiority. The manner in which he wheedles Heston into an interview—pretending to be an NRA member wanting to drop by for a friendly talk and filming—is a classic example. Another is the way he suckered his then-friend Larry Stecco into appearing in *Roger & Me*, then edited the footage to make Stecco, an attorney devoted to helping the poor, look like a spokesman for the brainless and wealthy.

7. LACKS EMPATHY, IS UNWILLING TO RECOGNIZE OR IDENTIFY WITH THE FEELINGS AND NEEDS OF OTHERS

This is not just a personal lack of empathy. The narcissist *simply cannot understand* when he has fouled up or put his foot in his mouth socially because he cannot understand that other people may see things differently. His feelings are the universe and the only reality.

Moore has a long and sordid history of posting screeds that make anyone with the smallest capacity for empathy immediately cringe. The narcissist would rather be notorious than be ignored. Take, as an example, his "Open Letter to Elian Gonzalez," a tirade that appeared on his web site during the 2000. In this case, he berates not Elian, but the mother who died trying to escape Cuba with him. She kidnapped him and placed his life in "horrible jeopardy," Moore writes to Gonzalez, adding, "The truth is your mother and her boyfriend snatched you and put you on that death boat because they simply wanted to make more money."

At times Moore's insensitivity has even alienated those who would otherwise be considered supporters. In an interview with FoxNews.com columnist Roger Friedman, "South Park" cocreator Matt Stone lamented Moore's cruel mistreatment of Charlton Heston in *Bowling for Columbine*: "It's hard to make Heston look sympathetic, but Moore did it. You can't help but think this is an 80-year-old man with Alzheimer's. He looked so frail."

Moore promptly responded: "[Heston] doesn't have Alzheimer's. He says he has Alzheimer's-like symptoms." *The New York Post* summed it up: "Moore doesn't quit while he's behind."

Precisely! This event and Moore's reaction to it are especially significant. We all frequently act out of self-interest; we all occasionally behave egocentrically or narcissistically. The difference is that we can perceive when we're behaving this way and retreat from dysfunction before it starts to define our personalities.

Moore's inability to recognize his own most egregious narcissistic lapses is very significant. Yes, Moore can't quit when he's behind—not out of stubbornness but because he doesn't see that he's screwed up royally. His view is the only view, and people simply *must* see that—or they fall into the "nation of idiots."

8. IS OFTEN ENVIOUS OF OTHERS OR BELIEVES THAT OTHERS ARE ENVIOUS OF HIM OR HER

In Moore's view, the world doesn't operate by cooperation, friendship, loyalty. It is comprised of rats clawing their way to the top, and to succeed, one must tear down the other rats. If someone gets hurt in the process – Larry Stecco, Charlton Heston, whoever—tough, they would have done the same. (Could it be coincidence that Moore named his film production firm "Dog Eat Dog Productions?")

Moore rarely misses an opportunity to profess his allegiance to his hometown of Flint, Michigan, yet he cannot hide his obvious pride at becoming a resident of a wealthy New York City neighborhood. He com-

With thanks to Dave Reddick

plained to the Onion AV Club that "[t]he local paper in Flint has never written the words, 'and he lives in a beautiful apartment on the Upper West
Side of Manhattan,' because the local paper in Flint hates me."

Yet in the same interview, Moore also explained how his new liberal
neighbors in New York are also jealous of his success. "They never mention
[the New York home] in Flint. But I'll read it in the liberal publications. . .
. They're just pissed because they're not sitting in this apartment." The writ-
ers of these articles, he adds, are "grunts" at *Newsweek* or the *New Yorker*,
and probably live in "a five floor walk-up down in the East Village." So,
continues Moore, "There's a voice in their head, the voice of class, screaming, [adopts whining voice] 'Not fair! Not fair!'"

Dr. Sam Vaknin outlines the essential envy component of narcissism:
"The suppression of envy is at the CORE of the narcissist's being. . . . If there
are others out there who are better than he – he envies them, he lashes out
at them ferociously, uncontrollably, madly, hatefully and spitefully."

Moore's long list of imagined rivals—the others he is constantly raging
against—include former Vice President Al Gore, President George Bush,
former NRA president Charlton Heston . . . not to mention the twelve pages
he spends in *Stupid White Men* just running down (in both senses of the
term) the current administration's Cabinet.

9. SHOWS ARROGANT, HAUGHTY BEHAVIORS OR ATTITUDES

Celebrities, once they reach a certain strata of fame, are often capable of
making income just by being celebrities. Moore is a classic example, as he's
now giving lectures to colleges across the country for tens of thousands a
pop.

Matt Hirsch, a Cornell student, saw this aspect of Moore when he
protested Moore's fee (then only $10,000) by presenting him with an over-
sized check in that amount, and pointed out that he'd charged more for a
few hours of time than some teaching assistants were paid in a year.

It was, if anything, a classic Moore stunt. But Moore exploded.
"Motherfucker. . . . You come down with your check making a big-ass statement," he shouted, according to the Cornell *Daily Sun*, "I give this money
away to organizations I support . . ."

Moore's rabid anger, and his attempt to humiliate the student, illustrates yet another related aspect of narcissism. "The narcissist is seething with enmity and venom," Dr. Vaknin points out. The venom can appear explosively when the narcissist is challenged. When Moore was criticized by a Florida congressman, he responded by hinting that the congressman might have played some part in the death of one of his female aides.

In another college appearance, this time at Humboldt State University in California, Moore was asked by a reporter about small businesses being taken over by chain stores.

Moore replied with a bombastic, deeply personal rant against small business, replying that in Flint small businesses "supported all the right-wing groups." Moore, the anticorporate activist, was on a roll. "The small hardware salesman, the small clothing store salespersons, Jesse the Barber who signed his name three different times on three different petitions to recall me from the school board. Fuck all these small businesses—fuck 'em all! Bring in the chains. The small businesspeople are the rednecks that run the town and suppress [sic] the people. Fuck 'em all."

This display indicates a truly pathological degree of self-absorption. That "Jesse the Barber" dared defy Moore in a piddling squabble thirty years before constitutes sufficient grounds to determine all issues relating to small businesses vs. chain stores.

One of the aspects of this haughtiness is the narcissist's feeling that he is above the law (the law is for *der untermensch!*) Moore's got that angle covered as well. The *New York Times* reported that, although Moore was famous for bothering others, he apparently didn't care for being bothered himself. After Moore fired Alan Edelstein, Edelstein took a play from Moore's playbook and began following Moore with a video camera, trying to corner him into an interview. "Mr. Moore responded by filing a complaint with the New York police accusing Mr. Edelstein of aggravated harassment, menacing and criminal trespassing," the *Times* article reported, and "As a result, Mr. Edelstein was arrested in March and spent nine hours in a cell at the Midtown North police station."

A narcissistic personality can have an even darker side, which Dr. Vaknin describes as a "burning desire, nay need, to be punished. In the grotesque mind of the narcissist, his punishment is equally his vindication. By being permanently on trial, the narcissist claims the high moral ground and the position of the martyr. . . ."

And Moore fits that bill. There's no question that he views his attacks on others (no matter how nasty or scurrilous) as a crusade, while others' criticism of him are character assassination and persecution.

Let's look again at a particularly conspicuous example: Moore's account of the police raid at his book-signing event for *Stupid White Men*. As Moore wrote, "I'm in San Diego, and I have just escaped being arrested by the San Diego police." He was signing books when he heard a commotion and saw people scattering. "The San Diego police are coming down the aisle, their large flashlights out [the auditorium lights are still on, so we all understand the implied "other" use of these instruments]." The officers begin shouting threats: "'VACATE THESE PREMISES IMMEDIATELY OR YOU WILL ALL BE ARRESTED!' I cannot believe what I am hearing. 'YOU WILL NOT RECEIVE ANOTHER WARNING. LEAVE NOW—OR FACE ARREST!'"

Moore attempts to reason with the brutish officers and is told "I don't care what you are doing—this is your last warning. I am ready to arrest you and everyone else."

Phew . . . in just a few paragraphs, Moore manages to expose a deep network of corruption and oppression brewing in the San Diego police department. Or is it that a larger force is at work—those nefarious henchmen of George W. Bush?

Unfortunately for Moore, one of the fans present at the event writes his own account, stating that he was astonished to read Moore's own description of the episode.

Kynn Bartlett gives a very different explanation of what happened. Sponsors of the book signing rented the auditorium until 11p.m. As the magic hour approached, the janitors pointed out that they had to stay late and clean things up, so punctuality would be appreciated. Imposing upon the working-class janitors was apparently of no concern to Moore, who according to Bartlett's account, kept on signing books after 11p.m. came and went. After a while the janitors got fed up with waiting and called the police, two of whom showed up.

Bartlett describes the affair after the police arrived. Two officers came in, "and rather decent ones at that, doing an uncomfortable task." They announced the use permit for the event had expired, and everyone had to leave. "The cops didn't come off as abusive, but rather as matter-of-fact and straight-forward," writes Kynn, "They didn't act like they were there to arrest droves of people for trespassing.

The incident illuminates several key signs of a narcissist. First, Moore has no concern for the janitors (who understandably want to get home before midnight). Second, he has no idea that this imposition on them might have consequences—they're just supposed to sit there and take it. Third, Moore takes any opportunity—or in this case, fakes any opportunity—to play the martyr. Two polite cops telling him his time is up and he has to leave become in Moore's mind a pair of thugs, out to threaten and imprison (or even beat) him and his followers. And the discrepancy between the two accounts shows how easily Moore will take a episode that seemed innocent to one of his fans, and spin it to play the persecuted martyr.

Ok, Mike, up off the couch. This session's on the house

CHAPTER 6

THIS MAN SPEAKS FOR THE DEMOCRATIC PARTY?

HERE is the man who sat next to Jimmy Carter at the Democratic National Convention. Here is the man Democrats under 30 most admire. Here is the man that Hollywood offers their highest praise and award. Here is the man the liberal leadership turns to for counsel and advice. Here is Michael Moore, in his own words.

"There is no terrorist threat in this country. This is a lie. This is the biggest lie we've been told."

And he's just getting warmed up...

"If someone did this to get back at Bush, then they did so by killing thousands of people who DID NOT VOTE for him! Boston, New York, D.C., and the planes' destination of California -- these were places that voted AGAINST Bush!"

– On September 11, 2001

"The Iraqis who have risen up against the occupation are not "insurgents" or "terrorists" or "The Enemy." They are the REVOLUTION, the Minutemen, and their numbers will grow -- and they will win."

"I'm sorry, but the majority of Americans supported this war once it began and, sadly, that majority must now sacrifice their children until enough blood has been let that maybe -- just maybe -- God and the Iraqi people will forgive us in the end."

"It's like an op-ed piece in the newspaper. These are my opinions. I'm very up front about them. I don't try and disguise them. I don't try to present them as objective news. They're not. They're very subjective."

– When asked if his movies were more like editorials than documentaries.

"Unfortunately, Bush and Co. are not through yet. This invasion and conquest will encourage them to do it again elsewhere. The real purpose of this war was to say to the rest of the world, "Don't Mess with Texas - If You Got What We Want, We're Coming to Get It!"

"I would like to apologize for referring to George W. Bush as a 'deserter.' What I meant to say is that George W. Bush is a deserter, an election thief, a drunk driver, a WMD liar, and a functional illiterate. And he poops his pants"

"I used to console myself about the state of stupidity in this country by repeating this to myself: Even if there are two hundred million stone-cold idiots in this country, that leaves at least eighty million who will get what I'm saying..."

– P. 85 of "Stupid White Men"

"Dumbest Brit here is smarter than the smartest American..."

– At London's Roundhouse Theater

"There's a gullible side to the American people. They can be easily misled. Religion is the best device used to mislead them."

"You know in my town the small businesses that everyone wanted to protect? They were the people that supported all the right-wing groups. They were the Republicans in the town, they were in the Kiwanas, the Chamber of Commerce - people that kept the town all white. The small hardware salesman, the small clothing store salespersons, Jesse the Barber who signed his name three different times on three different petitions to recall me from the school board. Fuck all these small businesses - fuck 'em all! Bring in the chains. The small businesspeople are the rednecks that run the town and suppress the people. Fuck 'em all. That's how I feel."

"White people scare the crap out of me. .... I have never been attacked by a black person, never been evicted by a black person, never had my security deposit ripped off by a black landlord, never had a black landlord ... never been pulled over by a black cop, never been sold a lemon by a black car salesman, never seen a black car salesman, never had a black person deny me a bank loan, never had a black person bury my movie, and I've never heard a black person say, 'We're going to eliminate ten thousand jobs here - have a nice day!'"

– In "Stupid White Men"

"Since September 11, the Bush Administration has used that tragic event as a justification to rip up our constitution and our civil liberties. And I honestly believe that one or two September 11s martial law will be declared in our country and we're inching towards a police state."

"The Patriot Act is the first step. "Mein Kampf" -- "Mein Kampf" was written long before Hitler came to power. And if the people of Germany had done something early on to stop these early signs, when the right-wing, when the extremists...decide that this is the way to go, if people don't speak up against this, you end up with something like they had in Germany. I don't want to get to that point."

"The motivation for war is simple. The U.S. government started the war with Iraq in order to make it easy for U.S. corporations to do business in other countries. They intend to use cheap labor in those countries, which will make Americans rich."

"We live in the time where we have fictitious election results that elects a fictitious president. We live in a time where we have a man sending us to war for fictitious reasons. Whether it's the fiction of duct tape or fiction of orange alerts we are against this war, Mr. Bush. Shame on you. Mr. Bush,

shame on you. And any time you got the Pope and the Dixie Chicks against you, your time is up."
– 2003 Academy Awards acceptance speech

"He is probably choking on a pretzel or something. I hope nobody tells him that I have won this award while he is eating a pretzel. ... He has the funniest lines in the film. I am eternally grateful to him."
– On President Bush after winning top prize at Cannes for Fahrenheit 9/11

While promoting his book, "Dude Where's My Country," in Germany, Moore gave a speech in which he asserted that, "Americans are possibly the dumbest people on the planet....in thrall to conniving, thieving, smug pricks. We Americans suffer from an enforced ignorance. We don't know about anything that's happening outside our country. Our stupidity is embarrassing."

"I want Bush paraded in handcuffs outside of a police house as a common criminal because I don't know if there's a greater crime than taking people to war based on a lie. I've never seen anything like Bush and his people. They truly hate our Constitution, our rights and our liberties. They have no shame in fighting for their corporate sponsors."
– Interview with *The Mirror*

"You're stuck with being connected to this country of mine, which is known for bringing sadness and misery to places around the globe."
– In England about America

"Should such an ignorant people [as the United States] lead the world? Don't go the American way when it comes to economics, jobs and services for the poor and immigrants. It is the wrong way."
– Open letter to the German people

CHAPTER 7

PROPAGANDA TACTICS AND FAHRENHEIT 9/11

DR. KELTON RHOADS is one of the nation's foremost authorities on the use of psychology and propaganda in modern culture. As a private-sector consultant and adjunct professor at the University of Southern California, Dr. Rhoads chose to analyze *Fahrenheit 9/11* not for any political reasons, but because he has an academic interest in propaganda. Here are some excerpts from his original paper on *Fahrenheit 9/11*, and if you are interested in the full version, you can obtain it at *www.workingpsychology.com/fahrenheit.html.*

PROPAGANDA TACTICS AND FAHRENHEIT 9/11
DR. KELTON RHOADS

I had my nose buried in books on the subject of propaganda analysis during June 2004, when Michael Moore's *Fahrenheit 9/11* was released. So it's embarrassing to admit I didn't immediately recognize something big was happening in my field, and that it was as close as my local theater: "feature-length movie-house agitprop," as one commentator called it, which he correctly recognized as "a relatively rare and new thing."

With a few notable exceptions, such as Leni Riefenstahl's work, propaganda has made a poor showing at the box office. Hollywood tried its hand at "message films" following World War II, but moviemakers soon discovered that people didn't go to theaters to have their consciences aggravated. Subsequent research has shown that individual movies rarely bring about major changes of opinion. Maybe that's why I was slow to see Moore's inferno.

Still—you'd think that a professor and psychological consultant who considers his expertise to be influence and persuasion, would have gotten to the theater sooner. But I finally did, and for those (admittedly few) of us who marvel at the virtuoso application of influence techniques, I'll say that *Fahrenheit 9/11* was a fine education.

Working in academia and the military, I have friends on the left and the right. To generalize: my left-looking friends tell me they think Moore accesses strong arguments but sometimes makes those arguments poorly; my right-leaning friends don't see how Fahrenheit could be persuasive to anyone but the deep left. So one of my goals in this paper is to illustrate to the Right the mechanisms operating behind Fahrenheit—how the film functions psychologically, and what it does to persuade.

To that end, I present eleven of the most favored psychological techniques from my study of propagandists the world over, and include portions of Moore's film that I believe illustrate those tactics. [In this abbreviated version of the paper, I present just four of these techniques and omit the references to save space. The full 14,000-word paper, with its 160+ endnotes, is available for download at http://www.workingpsychology.com.]

OMISSIONS

One of the most commonly employed propaganda techniques is the omission of relevant or truthful information that works against the propagandist's thesis. Some scholars consider omissions to be a form of deception; others argue that omissions are a normal part of human communication, which does not focus on background or contextual material for the sake of efficiency. Virtually everyone agrees that the intent of the commu-

With thanks to Dan Murphy, Artizans

nicator distinguishes deception from normal communication—an omission can be employed to intentionally give the wrong impression. Omissions ignore the contexts that may justify or undercut an action or idea; what gives them power is that they're often *not recognized as missing* by the audience.

Before we examine some key omissions, we need to explore that troubling "T" word: "Truth." How important are truthful or valid arguments in helping humans arrive at correct conclusions, anyway? Research has shown *the quality of an argument is largely irrelevant to humans.* Professor James Stiff, a leading judgment researcher, found a wimpy overall correlation between quality evidence and attitude change. He found that humans don't pay much attention to argument validity—rather, they pay attention to the argument's *claim or conclusion,* and how closely that claim or conclusion matches their prejudices. If a poorly argued message concludes with what a person already believes is true, he'll buy it. On the other hand, most powerfully reasoned arguments with ample supporting evidence will be rejected, if the conclusion doesn't match what the listener wants to hear.

Don't accuse humans of being logical—they're not. They're psycho-logical, which is something else entirely. That's why it's so common to see people giving faulty reasoning and invalid conclusions a pass: as long as the propagandist arrives at the "correct" conclusion, it really doesn't matter how he got there. Mere insinuation will serve about as well as solid evidence to prop up a prejudice.

We can hear this "psycho-logic" in the comment of a 20-year-old *Fahrenheit 9/11* devotee quoted in a *Los Angeles Times* article: "'I'm not a fan of the president,' one of the Times poll respondents said in an interview Thursday. 'If Michael Moore had done the film more truthfully, I would have been more impressed with it. But I agree with the main premise.'" The respondent gives Moore a pass on *truth,* because she agreed with his *claim* before setting foot in the theater. This is only human. And this helps explain why nearly a third of the respondents to the *Times* poll found *Fahrenheit 9/11* to be "completely accurate." Here are a few of the significant omissions in *Fahrenheit 9/11*:

In what Moore describes as one of the film's funniest moments, Moore ambushes congressmen, asking them to help him send their children to fight in Iraq. Republican Congressman Mark Kennedy gives Moore one of his best clips: a quizzical look that's used to humorous effect. What's cut, however, is Kennedy's response: "I have a nephew on his way to Afghanistan." According to the Star Tribune, Kennedy actually has two nephews in the military, and a son considering a career in the Navy. When Moore was charged with censorship for cutting Kennedy's response, he said that he deleted the clip because Kennedy didn't answer the question. If we got the impression that Republican Representative Michael Castle, who is shown walking and talking on a cell phone, was particularly desperate to avoid Moore, we may find it interesting that he doesn't have any children. And if we got the idea that it was primarily Republicans shirking their duties as patriotic parents, check the party affiliations of congressional parents who do have children in the military, listed in the full article.

Pre-war Iraq is shown as a peaceful haven, with Iraqi children playing on merry-go-rounds and flying kites, happy people eating in outdoor restaurants and smiling peacefully in sun-bathed plazas. Given Moore's view, it's no surprise we don't see gassed Kurds, mass burial fields, and dismembered Iraqi political prisoners. No dissenters hung from meat hooks, no torturing with blowtorches, vices, or drills. The sordid evidence from thirty years of Baathist war crimes, repression, and aggression are missing—they don't fit the thesis.

Moore portrays the Bush and Bin Laden families as close associates. Did you know that Osama can count 53 siblings in the family that disowned him in 1991? The rest of the large Bin Laden family has never been linked to terrorism, and has enjoyed a good relationship with the U.S. This, and other favorable relationships with the Bin Laden family are not examined, such as Jimmy Carter's successful solicitation of funds from several Bin Laden brothers for The Carter Center in 2000. Actually, let's stay with

Jimmy Carter for a moment—his brother Billy caused him some embarrassment, right? Did that make Carter any less of a president? No. Should it have? No.

Consider Republican icon Ronald Reagan. His son Ron speaks out on behalf of the Left. Does son Ron make father Ronald any less of a Republican? No. People in families are individuals. It's mentally lazy to generalize from a single family member to the entire family. Yet the propagandist can rely on the well-documented human propensity to jump from a single instance to a general indictment.

Moore capitalizes on a report (released by the White House during the Air National Guard "AWOL" flap) that expunged the name of a fellow Guard member by the name of James Bath. Bath is one of Moore's imputed conspirators, and a vital link between the Bush and Bin Laden families, as a money manager for one of the many Bin Laden brothers, Salem Bin Laden. Moore finds the crossed-out name to be a sinister attempt at deception, hiding evidence of the conspiracy implicating Bath, Bush, and the Bin Laden's. But Moore doesn't mention that 2003 federal law doesn't allow the National Guard to release medical information pertaining to other Guardsmen in a requested report, so they were bound by law to black out Bath's name in the version they released. Moore gloats about his investigative skill in obtaining an uncensored copy of the same report. It's merely a record released in 2000, before the privacy law of 2003 was in effect.

Past U.S. support for Saddam is highlighted and ridiculed. Not highlighted and ridiculed: that Saddam was a counterbalance to the U.S.'s greater enemy at the time, Ayatollah Khomeini of Iran. And, of course, there's not a word mentioned of the multiple UN resolutions that Saddam flouted.

For many, the most jarring omission was also the most obvious: the airplanes hitting the twin towers are not shown—only the dust and debris from the fallout, and the resulting human grief. The event inspiring the title of the movie—the definitive cause of the war—the encapsulating image—is missing. Although the film doesn't retreat from gore in other depictions,

With thanks to Larry Wright, The Detroit News

omitted here are the images of hopeless Americans jumping to their deaths, rather than suffocating from the smoke of the burning towers. Regarding America's feelings on 9/11, Moore had two primary emotions to play on: anger and sorrow, and he needed to offer his audience something to feel at this point in the film. He cleverly chose brooding sorrow over motivating anger with his choice of visuals. To dwell on anger and the desire for justice would not forward Moore's thesis of Afghanistan and Iraq as immoral and unjustified wars.

It's no wonder that omissions are one of the propagandist's most favored tools. Why burden the audience with information that will stop them from jumping to conclusions? Influence researchers sometimes refer to omissions as one-sided arguments. And the data show that they're great for "preaching to the choir," the true believers, or to the unaware and uninformed. On the other hand, one-sided arguments fare poorly with informed, educated, or skeptical audiences, who are aware that opposing arguments exist, and want to hear both sides pitted against each other. The sheer number of important omissions from *Fahrenheit 9/11* clues us into Moore's intended audience—or to Moore's misunderstanding of how one-sided arguments work, whichever may be the case.

An insight into Moore's mastery of omissions was observable in his July 28, 2004 interview with Bill O'Reilly, who's known for his badgering style. Moore insisted on two ground rules before interviewing with O'Reilly, and both of them were "tells," giving us insights into Moore's technique. First, Moore insisted that he be allowed to ask every other question in the interview. Moore (and every journalist) knows the person asking the questions has much more control over the interview, than the person answering them. That's why we see Moore asking lots of questions of his "marks" in his movies—it allows him to feed them lines or set them up with traps, just as it does for O'Reilly and thousands of other journalists. But more interesting was Moore's second request: he insisted that there be absolutely no editing of the video that was shot of the interview, not even editing for time. Why would he ask this? Video edits are one of Moore's primary weapons against his opponents. He's a master of cutting and splicing film so his interviewees look duplicitous or foolish. Aware as he was of the effectiveness of his own techniques, it's likely he didn't want them used against himself.

TRAPS

In my forthcoming book on propaganda, I call these E.W.Y.G.Y.S. traps: Either Way You Go You're Screwed. Traps are designed to embarrass a target regardless of what the target does or what positions they take.

Dan Greenburg wrote a humorous book, *How to Be a Jewish Mother*, which details the ways parents can control their children through shame and guilt. One of the tactics he recommends is that mothers give their children two shirts in a single gift box. The child opens the box, sees a green shirt and a blue shirt, and says, "Oh, Ma, what lovely shirts!" Mother says, "Try one of them on." The child tries on the green shirt. Mother says: "What, you don't like the blue one?"

Think about it: *most* actions can be arranged along a continuum of many possible responses. Whatever response is taken, the propagandist can point to some other point along the continuum and claim in the absence of evidence, or in hindsight, that it would have been a better solution. Then the propagandist manufactures social consensus so the unchosen option is seen as superior.

For example, Bush's opponents have the option of springing a simple but effective trap on the administration regarding future terror in the U.S. If the U.S. is terrorized again, opponents can use the event to castigate the administration's lack of effectiveness in securing the country. If the U.S. is *not* terrorized, opponents can minimize the impact of terrorism, and focus instead on Bush's extreme overreaction to 9/11 and the costs incurred for defending the country against an imagined threat.

Since a response to terror is filled with risk and unknown variables, any position taken can be sharply criticized. Thus, any sort of response to terror provides fodder for criticism and opportunities for more propaganda. Don't get me wrong; criticisms of current policy may be absolutely correct. But the use of traps where the critic has the advantage in both directions is disingenuous. Here are some of the traps that Moore sets in *Fahrenheit 9/11*:

> Bush ignored too many warnings about the terror that occurred, allowing citizens to die—and, on the other hand—Bush is issuing too many warnings about terror that hasn't materialized, manipulating us with fear.

> Bush was too rash in starting a war; Moore states elsewhere that there should be no war in Afghanistan—and, on the other hand—Bush waited too long before starting the war in Afghanistan, which allowed the terrorists to escape; Bush sat for 7 long minutes doing nothing after being told the second of the twin towers has been hit.

> Saddam was a big, dangerous problem that Bush missed—and, on the other hand—Saddam was not a problem because he was weak and ineffective.

> There's now too much security, intrusion, and encroachment on the personal liberties of U.S. citizens. Recall the three examples of harassed citizens in Moore's film: a group of cookie-munching peace activists, an elderly weightlifter, a mother and her baby hassled in the airport—and, on the other hand—there's need for more security in the airports (Moore wonders why cigarette lighters and matches aren't confiscated); Police in Oregon are underfunded, there's not enough security in the U.S.

> Too many U.S. soldiers are dying in Iraq and Afghanistan in an unjust war—and, on the other hand—we haven't sent enough U.S. troops into battle.

Bush should pursue Osama with less vigor or not at all (elsewhere, Moore demanded there be no war in Afghanistan; he opined that Osama should be considered innocent until proven guilty)—and, on the other hand—Bush should pursue Osama with more vigor (Bush has been distracted by Iraq;

Bush didn't send enough troops to Afghanistan quickly enough).

The Arabs need more freedom—and, on the other hand—the Arabs need more stability. (Don't we all?)

Bush is a bumbling fool—and, on the other hand—Bush is a master manipulator.

MODELING THE CONVERT COMMUNICATOR

A factual analysis of *Fahrenheit 9/11* only goes so far. For many, the movie leaves them with a *feeling* of truth. Humans being humans, we're likely to bank on our feelings, even when they contradict the evidence. It's our nature to give our emotions primacy over our intellect. So to stoke the emotional component of the film, Moore combines two potent tactics to good effect: Modeling, and the Convert Communicator.

First, *Modeling*: Humans are much more likely to perform a behavior if they see someone else performing it successfully. Psychologists call this process "modeling the behavior." It helps explain why we look in the direction that others are looking, buy books on Amazon that we see others buying, and jaywalk across the street when we see others doing it.

Albert Bandura, the famous clinical psychologist, created an entire therapy based on simple modeling. In one study, he was trying to resolve the phobias of children who were terrified of dogs. His therapy was nothing more than allowing these children to watch *other* children playing with a dog, either live or in film clips, for 20 minutes a day. After four days, over two-thirds of the formerly fearful children were willing to climb into a pen and remain confined with a dog, petting and playing with the animal. Remarkable, since none of these children were willing to do it four days earlier.

Another researcher has demonstrated there's a reliable increase in suicides after a suicide story hits the front pages of newspapers. It's merely another demonstration of the modeling effect. People are influenced by others regarding when to cross a street, when to be brave, whether to have an affair, and even when to die. So it comes as no surprise that the modeling effect can be harnessed for telling people how to vote.

The *Convert Communicator* is a special sort of model. Convert Communicators are often of low social status, and would not be considered persuasive under normal circumstances. But there's something a low status communicator can do to become spectacularly persuasive. They can reverse their positions! Convert Communicators are persuasive because they have converted dramatically from one ideology or lifestyle to an opposite one, and with that change can come an equally dramatic enhancement of credibility—and from credibility, persuasiveness.

Inside Alcoholics Anonymous, those who have spent the most years drinking, and have reformed, usually have the most status. A former felon, who has come clean and now uses his skills to combat robbery or computer fraud, is seen as extraordinarily knowledgeable and believable. Researchers have discovered that intravenous drug users found ex-drug users to be more credible than a physician, or the surgeon general of the United States!

Enter Moore's Convert Communicators. We are introduced to Marine Corporal Abdul Henderson as he stands in front of the capitol building. Here, he declares he would rather face a dishonorable discharge and serve jail time, than serve another tour of duty in Iraq. Leaving aside the extreme rarity of soldiers with these attitudes, Corporal Abdul Henderson provides us with an excellent example of the Convert Communicator. He's only a corporal, but his words have a powerful impact.

As the research shows, it doesn't take much status to become a forceful persuader, if one publicly renounces one's values and converts to the opposite point of view. Psychologists think the tactic works because we tend to attribute a change of heart to the power of the message. Humans normally try to be, or be seen as, consistent. We are inclined to think that only a powerfully truthful insight could cause a person to reverse their values, risk inconsistency, and convert to the opposite point of view.

Lila Lipscomb is the grieving mother whose appearance was called "the emotional center of the film" by the *Los Angeles Times*. She's introduced to us as a happy and confident woman, an ardent supporter of the U.S. military, and she says she used to detest Vietnam war protestors. She's religious, proudly flies the U.S. flag in front of her house, and identifies herself as a conservative Democrat. She's the model of a sympathetic heroine. Then we come to learn that she has lost a soldier son in Iraq: Michael Pedersen. As we experience her intense suffering, we apparently see her turning against the war and against Bush.

(Moore shot all these clips after her son's death, but the editing makes it appear as if the event is unfolding and Lila's bitterness is mounting.) In a scene of building emotion, Moore's cameras document Lila's disenchantment as she reads her deceased son's letters. Soon after, in perhaps the most touching scene in *Fahrenheit 9/11*, Moore's cameras record Lila's personal pilgrimage to Washington. A bystander, seeing the camera crew, scolds Lila for staging a conflict. Lila unloads on the bystander in a torrent of indignant emotion: "My son is not staged! My son is dead!" Our parting view of Lila shows her knees buckling in grief, her words choked with tears, as she finds a symbolic repository for all her pain and anger...the White House. For many, the scene is the most powerful in the movie. Then Moore segues in a voiceover: "I was tired of seeing people like Mrs. Lipscomb suffer." It's an odd comment coming from Moore, since *Fahrenheit 9/11* wouldn't have had the emotional punch it does, without capturing this heart-wrenching footage of Lila's grief.

One insightful commentator on this scene states correctly: "The power of Lipscomb's story lies in the sharpness of the U-turn she made." Moore's website posts the following quote regarding Lipscomb: "...she's a conservative, and that should be made note of. A conservative who believes the facts will reign." In the final scenes, it's clear that Lila's political position is fundamentally left and anti-war. But given Moore's proclivity for manufacturing persuasion, how certain are we that this represents a reversal for Lipscomb?

Was this really a conversion, or was the evidence arranged to make it look that way? Might we merely be watching Lila become more extreme in her preexisting convictions? We don't know Lipscomb's pre-war sentiments, but we make the assumption they're pro-war because she's pro-military. We do know, however, that her son Michael did not support the war as early as December 2002. In the film itself, Lila does not state that she supported the war in Iraq at any time.

Walking out of the theater, I was under the impression that she did initially support the war on Iraq, but several readings of Fahrenheit's script verified that I had invented Lipscomb's initial pro-war sentiment. Such is the propensity of the human mind to "fill in the gaps." Moore didn't force me to jump to the conclusion that Lipscomb originally supported the war before opposing it; I did that of my own accord. Perhaps other viewers did, too.

The power of the Convert Communicator comes from making a complete U-turn, not from becoming more of what one is already. So I'm not asking the same question that others have: "did Moore exploit or manipulate Lipscomb?" That speaks to interpersonal influence, not propaganda. My question is, did Moore exploit or manipulate us, the audience? Did he fake the U-turn? Was there really any turn at all, or are we actually viewing an Unconverted Communicator? We may never know for sure, but a bit of research turns up some of Lila's political positions:

- She voted for Bill Clinton.
- She voted for Al Gore.
- She declares: "Bush stole the presidency."
- Environmentally speaking, she says: "We've already destroyed the planet."
- She states she's impressed with Moore's other films.
- Regarding the mendacity of Moore's films, Lipscomb states: "Not one person has been able to stand up and say there has been one lie in this movie."
- Of Moore himself, she says, "Michael is a true visionary. I thank God that there are people like Michael Moore in the world."

Are these the words and positions of a conservative, a conservative Democrat, or a centrist? Or did Moore merely arrange for us to think we saw the necessary first leg of the U-turn, to utilize the tactic's persuasive power?

Readers who empathetically shared Lipscomb's grief may object to any examination of her positions. That objection is understandable: her status of bereaved mother, and Moore's ability to transmit her emotions to us, makes her an inviolate witness to war. Her feelings are beyond question or reproach. As the New York Times says, Lipscomb gives the film "an eloquence that its most determined critics will find hard to dismiss." This statement encapsulates the value of models providing highly emotional arguments: because they are felt, they can't be reasoned away. And this is why propagandists seek and cherish emotional arguments—in bypassing logic, they're as close to ironclad as an argument can get.

SHUTTING DOWN THE OPPOSITION

A good propagandist must not only tell his side of the story; he needs to shut down the opposition's ability to tell their side of it. Thus good propaganda is equal measures of offense and defense. Throughout the film, Moore has been playing offense. But after *Fahrenheit 9/11's* credits roll and the film is over, Moore continues to stoke the embers. The last blast from the *Fahrenheit 9/11* furnace is a strong defense cloaked as a counter-offense. Moore says he'll sue anyone who slanders his movie: "We want the word out. Any attempts to libel me will be met by force. The most important thing we have is the truth on our side. If they persist in telling lies, then I'll take them to court."

Moore has forewarned the public of a conservative counterattack (another good influence tactic), and has created a "war-room," fashioned after political quick-response teams, to defend the film's credibility. He's consulted with lawyers who can bring defamation suits against anyone who maligns the film or damages his reputation. Moore has hired a team of fact-checkers to defend the movie, but these employees caveat that they are not striving for reporter-level accuracy. They have relaxed the standards and are characterizing the film as an op-ed piece instead of factual reporting. Nonetheless, his lawyers defend its accuracy. "We have gone through every single word of this film—literally every word—and verified its accuracy," said his attorney, Joanne Doroshow.

The important thing here is that Moore remain on the attack. That's a good strategy. Social scientists Derek Rucker and Anthony Pratkanis have demonstrated how attacking others ("projection" is the term they use) reduces one's own appearance of guilt.

In their study, Rucker and Pratkanis allow an audience of subjects to watch three people (known creatively as A, B, and C) playing a competitive game. Pre-tests show that player B already looks suspicious to the audience. The researchers fuel these prejudices by telling their audience of subjects that player B will do anything to win. This allows the researchers to get off-the-charts levels of suspicion against player B, before the game begins. During the game, player B accuses the other two of cheating. In all of the replications of the experiment, player B's accusation effectively lowers his perceived culpability, and raises the appearance of guilt for players A and C! In some conditions, player B is able to get his levels of culpability lower than players A or C. Being the first to accuse others makes one look more innocent, according to the research. The results actually frustrated the researchers, because of the tactic's power: they couldn't find a way to stop the projection effect. Of course, this tactic has been used many times in human history.

One salient example is when Adolf Hitler accused the Poles of encroachment before he attacked them, and it gave Hitler cover at the time.

For his defense—or continued offense—Moore has hired former Clinton strategist Chris Lehane, known for his expertise in "opposition research," the art of discrediting opponents. Lehane's job is to respond to critics publicly. I've heard Lehane defending *Fahrenheit 9/11* on TV, and many of the tactics Lehane uses are pulled from the same pile as those enumerated above.

Is *Fahrenheit 9/11* documentary, or is it propaganda?

Call it as you will. For my part, I see a consistent, effective, and clever use of a range of established propaganda tactics. If only a few of these tactics were used, or if the attempt to deceive weren't as apparent, I might equivocate. But Moore has located many of the fundamental "bugs" in the human hardware, and capitalizes on them with skill. Michael Moore once said of his fellow Americans that "They are possibly the dumbest people on the planet." In *Fahrenheit 9/11*, it appears that he's counting on it. But the techniques Moore uses aren't exclusively effective on the American mind; *Fahrenheit 9/11* should be influential in other cultures as well.

Humans are, after all, humans. They're running cultural software over the same basic human hardware. For my own determination of whether Fahrenheit 9/11 is propaganda, I feel safe in applying the rule: if it flies, walks, swims, and quacks like a duck, it's a duck.

(Dr. Rhoads full paper with references is available at http://www.workingpsychology.com/fahrenheit.html)

CHAPTER 8

A FRAME BY FRAME DECONSTRUCTION OF FAHRENHEIT 9/11

NOBODY has written a better or more comprehensive deconstruction of Michael Moore's movie than Dave Kopel. Our movie highlighted several of his most important findings, and here we reprint a summary of his "59 Deceits" – the authoritative review of *Fahrenheit 9/11*. If you are intrigued by what you read here, we recommend a visit to www.davekopel.org and the Independence Institute to get the long version of "59 Deceits."

FIFTY-NINE DECEITS IN FAHRENHEIT 911
BY DAVID KOPEL, INDEPENDENCE INSTITUTE

If all you know is what the mainstream media tell you, then you are living in a world of illusions. But you can't free your mind if you merely replace one set of manipulative illusions with another set of manipulative illusions. Fahrenheit 9/11 is a twisted, dishonest, paranoid, and hateful fantasy. Learn the facts, and make up your own mind.

The list below is a summary of a much longer report, which is available for free at *www.davekopel.org. The report also discusses many other issues about the movie.*

There are lots of good reasons why people have chosen to vote against (or for) the re-election of George Bush. And there are lots of good reasons why patriotic Americans have decided to oppose (or support) the war in Iraq. One thing that all the good reasons have in common is that they are based on facts. In a democracy, we should try to convince our fellow citizens with facts and logical reasoning. To manipulate people with frauds and propaganda is to attack democracy itself.

1. The Gore "victory" rally isn't celebrating a Florida win. It was held before the polls had even opened.

2. Like all the other networks, Fox mistakenly said that Gore had won in Florida. The first network to retract the Florida mistake was CBS, not Fox.

3. A 6-month study by a consortium of major newspapers shows that Bush would have won the Florida recount under any of the terms which Gore sought in his lawsuits.

4. Investigation by the Palm Beach Post and others shows that race was not a reason why election officials mistakenly disqualified some voters because they were incorrectly thought to have felony convictions.

5. Bush's Presidency before 9/11 was not in serious trouble. No commentator said that he looked like a lame-duck president. Congress had passed his #1 bill (the tax cut) and was on the way to passing his #2 bill (the education bill). The scene at the end of the movie in which Bush tells a rich audience "I call you my base," was from an October 2000 charity fund-raiser. Both Gore and Bush spoke at the fund-raiser and, as is the custom at the fund-raiser, made fun of themselves.

With thanks to Oliver, CartoonWeb

6. "In his first eight months in office before September 11th, George W. Bush was on vacation, according to the Washington Post, forty-two percent of the time." As the Washington Post reported, the figure includes weekends, and includes time in "vacation locations" such as Camp David, where Bush was working—as when he met with Tony Blair.

7. In the golf course scene (about the middle of the movie), Bush had just heard about a terrorist attack on Israel. He called the press together to make a quick statement condemning the terrorism against Israel. He was not speaking about attacks on the United States.

8. There is no evidence that Bush did not read the Aug. 6, 2001 Presidential Daily Briefing about al Qaeda.

9. He never claimed that the title's "vagueness" was an excuse for not reading it.

10. The Briefing did not say "said that Osama bin Laden was planning to attack America by hijacking airplanes." It said that the FBI has "not been able to corroborate" such a threat.

11. The Saudis left the U.S. only after air travel was opened for the general public.

12. According to Richard Clarke and the September 11 Commission, Clarke personally approved the Saudi departures, and the decision went no higher in the chain of command.

13. Moore lied to a TV reporter in claiming that Fahrenheit discloses Clarke's decision to the audience. Clarke called the Saudi exit material in Fahrenheit a "mistake" by Moore.

14. Contrary to what Fahrenheit claims, the September 11 Commission found that many Saudis were asked "detailed questions" before being allowed to leave.

15. James Bath did not invest bin Laden family money in Bush's energy company Arbusto. He invested his own money.

16. Bath's name was blacked-out from an Alabama National Guard record released by the White House—as required by federal law, which prohibits the disclosure of health-related personal information.

17. Prince Bandar has way too much influence on the U.S. government, as Fahrenheit shows, but American coddling of the Saudi tyranny is a long-standing bi-partisan tradition, not a Bush invention.

18. Harken Energy: Bush only sold the stock after company lawyers told him it was OK.

19. The reason that Bush "beat the rap" was because there was no evidence he had engaged in insider trading.

20. The Carlyle Group is not a Bush playground. Many Bush opponents are investors, including George Soros.

21. The Bush administration dealt Carlyle a huge financial blow by canceling the Crusader missile, one of the few weapons cancellations in the Bush administration.

22. The bin Ladens dropped out of Carlyle before the stock sale. Of the $1.4 billion that the Saudis invested in companies with Bush connections, the vast majority of the money was invested in Carlyle before George H.W.

Bush joined the firm.

23. Craig Unger claims that the Saudis have $860 billion invested in the U.S. The figure appears in his book House of Bush, House of Saud, but neither of Unger's cited sources support such a large figure.

24. Moore claims that the Saudis "own 7% of America." But even if you believe Unger's fictitious $860 billion figure, the Saudis own only about 7% of total foreign investment in America, which is over 10 trillion dollars. Only if all of America were owned by foreigners could Moore's claim be correct.

25. The Saudi embassy does not receive special protection. It is not the only foreign embassy which is guarded by the U.S. Secret Service. An international treaty signed by the U.S. requires the U.S. to protect any embassy which asks for protection.

26. Moore's insinuation that Bush runs U.S. foreign policy according to Saudi instructions is contradicted by the Afghanistan invasion (which toppled the Taliban regime which the Saudis strongly supported), and by the Iraq War (which the Saudis opposed, in part because Iraqi oil will compete with Saudi oil).

27. As Governor of Texas, Bush never met with Taliban representatives.

28. The proposed Unocal pipeline was supported by the Clinton administration, but Unocal abandoned the pipeline idea in 1998.

29. The new Afghani government has signed a protocol to build a pipeline, but it is an entirely different pipeline, in a location hundreds of miles distant from the Unocal proposal.

With thanks to Gary Waltrip, ChronWatch

30. Construction has not begun on the new pipeline. Although Moore claims that "Enron stood to benefit" from the pipeline, Enron has never had any participation in either pipeline.

31. The Bush administration did not "welcome" Taliban diplomats in March 2001, but instead condemned them for failing to hand over Osama bin Laden.

32. Despite Moore's pose in the movie, he opposed the Afghanistan War, and—in December 2002—claimed that Osama bin Laden might be innocent.

33. In claiming that the Afghanistan invasion was a mere ruse to protect the Saudis, Moore omits the results of liberation in Afghanistan: destruction of al Qaeda training camps, the creation of free elections, more freedom for women, and the homecoming of 1.5 million refugees from the Taliban.

34. The various quotes about Bush administration cooperation with the September 11 Commission have been resequenced to create a false impression.

In July 2003, Chairman Kean complained about lack of cooperation. In February 2004, Bush said that the White House had given extraordinary cooperation. Kean agreed, and praised the White House for providing "unprecedented" access.

35. John Ashcroft didn't really lose a Senate election to a "dead guy." Mel Carnahan died in a plane crash a few weeks before the election, and the Missouri Governor had promised to appoint Carnahan's widow Jean Carnahan if voters pulled the lever for Mel Carnahan.

36. The FBI did not "know" about al Qaeda suspects who were attending flight training schools. The information was never passed above the level

of one field office.

37. Ashcroft did not cut overall counter-terrorism funding. He only proposed a one-year cut in a particular program that already had two years of unspent money.

38. Rep. Porter Goss says he has an "800 number," and the Fahrenheit caption says "He's lying." Goss does have a tollfree number, although the prefix is 877.

39. Moore say Saddam's Iraq "had never murdered a single American citizen." In fact, Saddam paid for terrorist bombers in Israel who murdered Americans, along with people of other nationalities. Saddam also sheltered the American-killing terrorist Abu Nidal, and the bomb-maker for the 1993 World Trade Center bombings.

40. In addition, Saddam ordered assassination attempts against former President Bush and against U.S. diplomats in the Philippines.

41. Moore claims that the Saddam regime "never threatened to attack the United States." In fact, in 1997 the regime publicly ordered: "American and British interests, embassies, and naval ships in the Arab region should be the targets of military operations and commando attacks by Arab political forces." On the first anniversary of September 11, Saddam's regime called for suicide attacks on Americans.

42. Moore claims that there was no connection between Iraq and al Qaeda. In fact, there is an extensive record of collaboration although—as the September 11 Commission announced—there is no proof that Saddam participated beforehand in al Qaeda attacks on America.

43. Fahrenheit shows Condoleezza Rice saying, "Oh, indeed there is a tie

between Iraq and what happened on 9/11." The audience laughs derisively. Here is what Rice really said on Nov. 28, 2003:

> "Oh, indeed there is a tie between Iraq and what happened on 9/11. It's not that Saddam Hussein was somehow himself and his regime involved in 9/11, but, if you think about what caused 9/11, it is the rise of ideologies of hatred that lead people to drive airplanes into buildings in New York. This is a great terrorist, international terrorist network that is determined to defeat freedom. It has perverted Islam from a peaceful religion into one in which they call on it for violence. And they're all linked. And Iraq is a central front because, if and when, and we will, we change the nature of Iraq to a place that is peaceful and democratic and prosperous in the heart of the Middle East, you will begin to change the Middle East...."

44. Moore portrays pre-liberation Iraq as a happy nation of kite-flying and weddings. In fact, a sixth of the population had fled Saddam's tyranny. The United Nations and Amnesty International condemned "the systematic, widespread and extremely grave violations of human rights and of international humanitarian law by the Government of Iraq, resulting in an all-pervasive repression and oppression sustained by broad-based discrimination and widespread terror."

45. The only Iraqi casualties which Moore shows are civilians, although military casualties far outnumbered civilian.

46. When showing pictures of buildings being blown up, Moore does not reveal that many of them were military buildings, and civilians were never allowed anywhere near them.

47. A humorous sequence making fun of tiny countries in the Iraq libera-

tion Coalition does not even mention the major countries in the Coalition, such as the U.K., Australia, Italy, and Japan.

Not a deceit, but mean-spirited and exploitive: The footage of the funeral of U.S. Air Force Maj. Gregory Stone at Arlington National Cemetery appears without his family's permission, and over their vehement objection. Major Stone strongly believed in the Iraq mission, as does his family. The footage of Massachusetts National Guardsman Peter Damon, who is undergoing therapy at Walter Reed Army Medical Center is also used without his permission.

48. Despite Moore's claims, American media have not been mindlessly supportive of the Iraq war. For example, Peter Jennings has been extremely critical. The evidence that Moore offers to portray Jennings as a war supporter is a clip of Jennings reporting in April 2003 that Saddam's army had collapsed—which was true.

49. The scene of American soldiers making fun of a man underneath a sheet is not torture of a prisoner of war. They are making fun of a drunk who passed out in the street.

50. Moore reports that Bush proposed closing some Veteran's hospitals. But he also proposed opening other veteran's hospitals.

51. Bush once opposed renewing a special bonus of $75/ month for soldiers in "imminent danger zones." Moore claims that Bush proposed cutting combat soldiers' pay by 1/3; but a soldier's pay and benefits is over $27,000 per year, even at low enlisted grades.

52. While making false claims about a Bush pay cut, Moore omits the fact that Bush sought and won a 3.7% military pay raise in 2003.

53. Moore claims that only one Congressman has a child in Iraq. Actually, two do. (Democratic Senator Tim Johnson of S.D., and Republican Rep. Duncan Hunter of California.) Also, John Ashcroft has a son on a naval ship in the Persian Gulf.

54. *Fahrenheit 9/11* deceptively cut the footage of Rep. Mark Kennedy to make it look like Kennedy rebuffed Moore's request to help enlist Congressional children. In fact, Kennedy said it was a good idea, and offered to help.

55. *Fahrenheit 9/11* shows Rep. Michael Castle walking past Moore. But Rep. Castle is childless.

56. Based on Census Bureau data, Congressional families are more likely than other families to have children serving in Iraq.

57. Moore calls Flint, Michigan, "my hometown." In fact, he grew up in Davison, a much wealthier and much whiter suburb.

58. In *Fahrenheit 9/11*, Moore pretends to support our troops. But in fact, he supports the enemy in Iraq-the coalition of Saddam loyalists, al Qaeda operatives, and terrorists controlled by Iran or Syria-who are united in their desire to murder Iraqis, and to destroy any possibility of democracy in Iraq. Here is what Moore said on April 14, 2004, about the forces who are killing Americans and trying to impose totalitarian rule on Iraq: "The Iraqis who have risen up against the occupation are not 'insurgents' or 'terrorists' or 'The Enemy.' They are the REVOLUTION, the Minutemen, and their numbers will grow—and they will win." Do you really think that someone who wants Iraq to be ruled by Islamist or Ba'athist tyranny, and who deliberately kills innocent civilians with car bombs, is like the American Minutemen?

59. As reported in the trade journal Screen Daily, affiliates of the Iranian and Syrian-backed terrorist group Hezbollah are promoting *Fahrenheit 9/11*, and Moore's Middle East distributor, Front Row, is accepting the terrorist assistance: "In terms of marketing the film, Front Row is getting a boost from organizations related to Hezbollah which have rung up from Lebanon to ask if there is anything they can do to support the film. And although [Front Row's Managing Director Giancarlo] Chacra says he and his company feel strongly that Fahrenheit is not anti-American, but anti-Bush, 'we can't go against these organizations as they could strongly boycott the film in Lebanon and Syria.'" (Nancy Tartaglione, "Fahrenheit to be first doc released theatrically in Middle East," Screen Daily.com, June 9, 2004. The story is discussed in Samantha Ellis, "*Fahrenheit 9/11* gets help offer from Hezbollah," The Guardian (London), June 17, 2004.)

CHAPTER 9

WHY NO MENTION OF ISRAEL IN YOUR MOVIE, MICHAEL?

"It's all part of the same ball of wax, right?
The oil companies, Israel, Halliburton."
– Michael Moore

You probably don't read *Screen Daily*, unless you're in the movie business. But if you do read it you can keep up on how the terrorist group Hezbollah, which has kidnapped and murdered hundreds of Americans and Israelis and abets Al Qaeda, is using Michael's film.

Hezbollah has put *Fahrenheit 9/11* into service training a new generation of terrorists. That's because Michael Moore has called Iraqi insurgents "noble Minutemen" and branded U.S. soldiers evil brutish simpletons. So the film is no different from what Arabs are used to seeing. Except that *Fahrenheit 9/11* is far more persuasive to impressionable Arabs because it comes from an American.

When questioned about this Hezbollah connection by the media, Michael initially denied any connection. Then, when hit with the facts, he stonewalled. This man who spends so much time getting in other people's faces was not willing to explain the details of his connection with

Hezbollah. So we'll step in and provide the service.

Michael Moore's vocal opinions about Israel go back to 1990 when he was one of the speakers at a June 5th demonstration denouncing Israeli occupation of West Bank and Gaza. Over time, his position on Israel intensified. In *Dude, Where's My Country?* Michael offered his solution to the Middle East crisis:

> **"Give the Palestinians a bunch of missile-firing Apache helicopters and let them and the Israelis go at each other head to head. Four billion dollars a year to Israel – four billion dollars a year to the Palestinians – they can just blow each other up and leave the rest of us the hell alone."**

Michael dedicated *Dude Where's My Country?* to Rachel Corrie, an International Solidarity Movement volunteer who was killed March 16 when she climbed atop a bulldozer that was destroying tunnels used by Palestinian terrorists to smuggle weapons from Egypt into Gaza. And what else did Michael write in that clever book of his?

> **"Of course many Israeli children had died too, at the hands of the Palestinians. You would think that would make every Israeli want to wipe out the Arab world, but the average Israeli does not have that response. Why? Because in their hearts, they know they are wrong, and they know they would be doing just what the Palestinians are doing if the sandal were on the other foot."**

When Michael cannot find any moral difference between Israeli policies and Palestinian policies, the urge is to grab him and shake him and ask if he's forgotten those scenes on the West Bank after 9/11 when Palestinians who took to the streets to celebrate the atrocities.

With thanks to Gary Waltrip, ChronWatch

But despite his apparent anti-Semitic views, Michael was careful not to use the world "Israel" in *Fahrenheit 9/11* – not even once. He even edited it out of a speech clip he used with President Bush. Now why would he do that? Could it be that he knows a lot of Jews are registered Democrat and he didn't want them to know how he really feels about Israel, and about Jews? Given the mendacity of his views, this has the ring of truth!

CHAPTER 10

OUR FIRST FILM REVIEW – WRITTEN WHILE WE WERE STILL FILMING!

THE HYPE STOPS HERE
A REVIEW OF FAHRENHYPE 9/11

The stupefying success of Michael Moore's *Fahrenheit 9/11* has spawned a raft of similar political films, but only one rebuttal. Titled *FahrenHYPE 9/11*, this rebuttal parades a who's who of political prizefighters into the cinematic ring in a much more reverential retelling of the tragedy that shook a nation.

In Moore's dreamy recollection of the 2000 presidential race in Florida, we are led to believe that the TV networks called the election for Gore but then changed their minds after FOX called Bush the victor. It's a silly premise on it's face, sillier when investigated. *FahrenHYPE 9/11* takes us behind the headlines and shows us how every credible post-election analysis, despite how liberals have convinced themselves otherwise, concluded that Bush won Florida fair and square.

Indeed, if there is any conspiracy theory worth its mettle, consider this one: The networks tried to tilt the election to Gore by calling the election before the polls closed in the conservative panhandle of the state, discouraging voters in an area that was heavily Bush country. Think about it!

Painting Moore as the Grand Prevaricator from the getgo, *FahrenHYPE 9/11* resists the temptation of simply answering Moore's claims and instead takes us behind the scenes of the events leading up to 9/11. And who better to lead the storytelling than Dick Morris, savvy imagemeister to both Republicans and Democrats, including to Bill Clinton for 25 years. Morris brings an insider perspective that is instantly refreshing and startling.

To tell the whole story of 9/11, Morris recalls in intimate detail how Clinton had six opportunities to take out Osama, and why in each case he let Osama go. For people like Michael Moore who are eager to pin 9/11 on the Bush Administration, this like-you-were-there account of Clinton's 8-year record against terror may cause you to question the very premise of Michael Moore's movie, much less whether it's all hype.

Anybody who has seen *Fahrenheit 9/11* – and some 20 million of us have – knows Mr. Moore takes a propagandist's license in shuffling facts to create the version of "truth" he seeks. That's his privilege. Equal privilege must go to *FahrenHYPE 9/11* for pointing out what most thinking liberals are too cowed to admit but lifelong Democrat Ed Koch has no trouble in saying: "Michael Moore is a dog." Perhaps a cross between mastiff and pitbull.

FahrenHYPE 9/11 is no Bush apologist. It pins blame for 9/11 in historically appropriate measures: eight years to Clinton, eight months to Bush. But rather than dwell on past mistakes, the focus is on the polarization of politics in America and the very different choices offered by the two political parties.

Running through this movie from start to finish is the question: Is our nation safer with the turn-the-other-cheek policies of Michael Moore's Democratic Party, or are we safer with the take-charge, take-names policies of George Bush's Republican Party?

In one of the most startling revelations of the movie, we learn how

With thanks to Gary Waltrip, ChronWatch

Saddam Hussein lavished $10,000,000,000 – yes, ten billion dollars in bribes to top officials of France, Germany and Russia in exchange for their vetoes on the U.N. Security Council. We see America's allies stuck between the American rock and a Muslim hard place. And we begin to wonder if our allies are really our allies, and if trying to work with them will ever yield results.

FahrenHYPE 9/11 makes few distinctions between Moore, Kerry or Clinton – labeling all liberal. Given that Kerry has tacitly or surreptitiously allowed Moore to serve as his attack dog, it's not unfair to conclude that Moore's movie has the liberal stamp of approval.

The hole in lower Manhattan that still haunts our nation is put in stark contrast to Moore's odd claims, such as those make in a speech in Berlin, that "There is no terrorist threat – it's a lie, it's the biggest lie we've been told."

Rather than indulge Moore his oddities, however, *FahrenHYPE 9/11* seeks the higher ground – as the saying goes, never argue with a fool, people may not know the difference – and we soon depart New York on an answer-seeking excursion. Once again, expect to be surprised by the landscape revealed in *FahrenHYPE 9/11* – it bares little resemblance to the sanitized, politically-correct nightly news. Some segments are presented so very differently than you're accustomed to seeing on the nightly news that you may at first be suspect of its veracity – except that all is carefully documented on screen. As Dick Morris says, "if you've swallowed Moore's poison, this is the antidote."

FahrenHYPE 9/11 takes umbrage at Moore's portrayal of U.S. soldiers as nutheads and whack cases who don't trust their President (need a mirror, Michael?). We hear from GI's who have been to Iraq, as well as those preparing to go – the movie captures them at their most honest – neither as the "cannon fodder" of Moore's portrayal nor the "warrior dolls" of Pentagon choosing, but intensely passionate young Americans who recognize that they're walking point for their generation's fight against a new kind of enemy.

While applauding a country that allows and even encourages a Moore, *FahrenHYPE 9/11* is all about evening the score and setting the record straight. One scene after another of Moore's movie is dissected, laid open and revealed as a sham wrapped in garlic hidden in an enema:

Soldiers supposedly abusing Iraqi prisoners is a *fabrication*.

Congressmen refusing to send their boys to war is a *misrepresentation*.

Bush attacking Iraq solely for oil and self-interest is an *allusion*.

If anything rankles the makers of *FahrenHYPE 9/11*, it is the gullibility of today's movie-going audience. That the hard left swallows Moore's movie as the gospel truth, or hard conservatives spit it out in disgust, doesn't concern here. What concerns are all of the mainstream Americans who are rethinking their opinions on Bush because they believe Moore's movie is documentary fact.

Not polemic, fact. Not propaganda, fact.

"Bush lied about WMDs" appears in a Google search almost as often as "Janet Jackson's breast" and in today's celeb-idolizing culture, that's saying a mouthful.

"Michael Moore has proof," people say in their Sunday earnest. Meanwhile you can just hear Moore chuckling all the way to the bank. He even told CNN's Lou Dobbs that "it's a comedy... how can there be inaccuracies in comedy?" Yet the people bite—hook, line and stinker. One empowered individual with a camera can wreak a lot of havoc with the right hype in today's world.

Moore hits bulls-eye in a Florida classroom on 9/11. George Bush is shown reading to children and then looking rather stupid for several minutes, just sitting there after being told by aides that America is under attack. The image impressed in people's minds is one of Bush incapable of command, a puppet needing Dick Cheney's string-pulling. What Mr. Moore doesn't show in his clearly doctored footage is anything vaguely approaching the truth of that day. (Ever wonder why NBC, ABC, CBS, CNN et al didn't show any footage of the event on the evening news of September 11th?)

FahrenHYPE 9/11 spends time with the senior reporter who was in the classroom that day, and with the principal of the school who was also there, to get the accurate truth of the day – something Moore and the Democratic Party leadership surely wish you won't see. If the truth can hurt, it can also heal.

To respond to Mr. Moore's most absurd conspiracies, *FahrenHYPE 9/11* calls out the right wing's foxy firebrand, Ann Coulter. She rips into Moore with obvious glee. Her assessment of why Moore made his film, and the glaring Democratic Party deficiency that Moore is trying to laugh away, is explosive stuff.

Eager to present a balanced attack on Mr. Moore, the movie also pays a visit to Young Harris in the mountains of Georgia, home to elder statesman Zell Miller. With his two Labs under foot, Senator Miller talks about his lifelong devotion to the Democratic Party and the principles of FDR, Truman, and Kennedy. But for the first time in his life, he is voting for a Republican for President. The Senator laments how once fringe players like Michael Moore have hijacked his Party and turned it into an Abba sit-in.

Perhaps most poignant in *FahrenHYPE 9/11* is Congressman Peter King's remembrance of 9/11. His District is Long Island. He lost over 100 constituents that day. He gave the eulogies for two firemen who rushed into the towers. Time has passed, now, but the salt that Michael Moore has rubbed into the hot wounds of victims' families leaves a bitter sting. Mr. Moore is advised not to show his face in King's Parrish. How could anyone, his constituents wonder, so underhandedly attack a President who's doing his best to fight the terrorists who destroyed their loved ones?

Great documentaries take you where you weren't supposed to go, and *FahrenHYPE 9/11* is the first to take you behind the gears and trappings of the Official 9/11 Commission and Department of Homeland Security. Here's a stark portrayal of dozens of terrorist attacks that have happened

With thanks to Cox & Forkum

since 9/11 that you know nothing about – because they were thwarted!

Gazing up at the vulnerable underbelly of the Brooklyn Bridge, once one of the great wonders of the world, we learn how U.S. counterterrorism forces uncovered a bomb plot in progress and foiled it in time – before hundreds more New Yorkers would have perished. Even more compelling are the methods the FBI used to capture the terrorist – and *FahrenHYPE 9/11* tells all, leaving nothing to the ellipses like the movie it answers.

Other icons of American success, from Citibank to the World Bank, were similarly targeted in the weeks and months after 9/11. Detailed plans were hatched to "let the bodies pile up in bags" by the tens or even hundreds of thousands. But those plots were thwarted, and we see how.

Then there's Las Vegas, South Beach, Northern Virginia, Columbus – all places far from New York but not safe from terrorism. Terrorists had identified hard targets in these places, and were ready to strike with the lethal force of Stinger missiles, biological warfare, and radioactive dirty bombs. But none of these plans came to pass. Why?

FahrenHYPE 9/11 credits Bush for keeping terrorists on the run, disrupting operations, drying up funds, and not just taking the easy way out but flat declaring what the majority of Americans feel in their hearts: "all terrorist rogue nations are enemies of the U.S. and we'll take this war to your shore – we won't just sit back and take it!"

Today there are big block letters filling the upper windows of a building overlooking Ground Zero -- "NO WAR". It's a bold pronouncement and *FahrenHYPE 9/11* helps us all answer the obvious question: If not war, then what? Peace, presumably. And how is that peace achieved?

By denying that millions of Arabs wish the wrath of Allah upon us and intend to keep trying to kill as many of us as possible?

By playing nice with Arabs and deserting Israel...when Arab hatred stems clearly from the bald contrast of our culture's success to their abject failure?

By focusing only on Osama—taking him out and getting back to our lives…when Osama is but a catalyst for a festering contagion and other Osama's will rise up and someday use WMDs against us?

By thinking that our attacking Iraq only helps terrorist's training efforts… when this same argument was made when Clinton fired missiles into Somalia and Afghanistan and the terrorists continued about their business?

By waiting for our so-called allies to come to our aid…when their societies are being overrun by disaffected Muslims and their leaders view appeasement as policy and Saddam's bribes as gravy?

By joining hands with Islamic radicals and all singing Kumbaya and asking the universal consciousness to implore peace upon all mankind?

Wishful thinking and good intentions aren't going to bring back 3,000 innocents, or save the next 3,000 or 300,000…as much as we all wish it were possible. That is the ultimate message of *FahrenHYPE 9/11*, the message that we must all wrestle with in this election year and beyond.

Lee Troxler
September 2004